On Retreat

Exploring
the Fruit of the Spirit

Copyright © 2025 Dale Jones and Alison Tye

All rights reserved. No portion of this book may be reproduced, stored in a retrieval system, or transmitted in any form or by any means – electronic, mechanical, photocopy, recording, scanning, or other – except for brief quotations in critical reviews or articles, without the prior written permission of the authors. For contact information, visit: http://www.awakenretreats.com.au.

ISBN: 978-0-9954286-9-0

Unless otherwise indicated, all Scripture quotations are taken from the Holy Bible, New Living Translation, copyright © 1996, 2004, 2015 by Tyndale House Foundation. Used by permission of Tyndale House Publishers, Carol Stream, Illinois 60188. All rights reserved.

Scripture quotations marked MSG are taken from *The Message*, copyright © 1993, 2002, 2018 by Eugene H. Peterson. Used by permission of NavPress. All rights reserved. Represented by Tyndale House Publishers.

Scripture quotations marked (NIV) are taken from the Holy Bible, New International Version®, NIV®. Copyright © 1973, 1978, 1984, 2011 by Biblica, Inc.™ Used by permission of Zondervan. All rights reserved worldwide. www.zondervan.comThe "NIV" and "New International Version" are trademarks registered in the United States Patent and Trademark Office by Biblica, Inc.™

Scripture quotations marked TPT are from The Passion Translation®. Copyright © 2017, 2018, 2020 by Passion & Fire Ministries, Inc. Used by permission. All rights reserved. ThePassionTranslation.com.

Some content taken from The Hidden Life by Kitty Crenshaw and Catherine Snapp. Copyright © 2006. Used by permission of NavPress, represented by Tyndale House Publishers, a Division of Tyndale House Ministries. All rights reserved.

Cover design by Steven Tye.

To those who have shown us a contemplative way of life and guided us to a deeper relationship with Christ – through their writing, their poetry, their lives and the relationships they have shared with us.

In your freedom:
Walk by *the Spirit*
Live by *the Spirit*
Keep in step with *the Spirit*
Bloom in the fruit of *the Spirit*

CONTENTS

Why Retreat? 1
How To Use This Book 2
The Fruit Of The Spirit 4
Love 7
Joy 22
Peace 42
Patience 57
Kindness 76
Goodness 90
Faithfulness 106
Gentleness 125
Self-control 140
Lectio Divina 161
The Prayer of Examen 163
Imaginative Bible Reading 165
Suggestions For Group Leaders 167
Suggestions For Individuals 171
Notes 174
About the Authors 178

WHY RETREAT?

"A spiritual retreat is never simply a matter of rest or relaxation, planning or even teaching. Its focus is relational. It is centered on encountering God. A spiritual retreat is a time to set aside all our agendas, attachments and preoccupations and place ourselves completely in the hands of God. It is a response to an invitation from our heavenly Father to come away with him."

— *Juliet Benner, Contemplative Vision (2011)* [1]

When we come away on retreat, even just for a day, we make the choice to separate ourselves from our normal lives and to be open and attentive to the Holy Spirit.

A retreat is an opportunity to slow down, to spend time with God in silence and solitude, and to pay attention, to listen, and to notice where He may be speaking to us. It's a time to gently set aside all our "stuff" and to place ourselves in the hands of God. It's our response to an innate longing to spend time alone with and listening to the Divine. And when we gather as a group, we also come together in community – as a group of people prayerfully supporting and upholding each other.

In our world of constant hurry and concern with productivity, taking time for retreat is counter cultural, but we know that everything Jesus came to share also went against the norm. So, we intentionally set aside time to focus our hearts on God, to ground ourselves in the present moment and to seek His voice with both anticipation and expectation.

How To Use This Book

Each of the fruit of the Spirit presented in this book can be explored as a separate day retreat by groups or individuals. Each fruit is broken into three parts and as a suggestion, a group day retreat following our outlines could be structured as follows:

8:30am	Arrive together
8.45am	Introduce the topic and group members
9am	Part 1
10.30am	Morning tea
11am	Part 2
12.30pm	Lunch
1.30pm	Part 3
3pm	Afternoon tea
3.30pm	Group reflection
4.30pm	Finish

This plan can be adapted for individuals. If it is not possible to spend a whole day away on retreat, then parts one, two and three of each fruit of the Spirit could be utilised as shorter pieces for individual reflection or used as stimulus within contemplative prayer groups.

As you follow the outline for each fruit of the Spirit, you will need:
- A pen or a pencil.
- A journal or notebook. Some lined pages are provided for note taking; however, you may wish for more space than what is

provided.
- A way to listen to music.
- A quiet space on your own.
- A Bible.

Some sections of this book invite you to engage in contemplative practices such as Lectio Divina, The Prayer of Examen or imaginative Bible reading. If you are unfamiliar with these practices, an overview is provided towards the end of the book for your reference. Each of these practices can also be extended for use outside of the reflections in this series.

A link is provided for each song that is referenced. Scan the QR code to access the music via YouTube.

Our deep joy is to see people exploring, growing and nurturing their relationship with God. We pray that through this retreat series, you might know and experience God's great love for you.

THE FRUIT OF THE SPIRIT

"Greetings you who are highly favoured. The Lord is with you. Blessed is she who has believed that the Lord would fulfill his promises to her!"

Luke 1:28, 45 (NIV)

These words were spoken to Mary, mother of Jesus and we believe Jesus wants to speak these same words to us today. We are highly favoured by God - made in His image. Part of His favour is gifting us with His presence, His Spirit.

In the lead up to His death, Jesus told His friends that it was for their good that He was going away, because until He left, the Holy Spirit would not come to them. The Holy Spirit was Jesus' gift to His friends - the advocate, the comforter - one to lead us "into all truth".

During this series of retreats our focus will be on the fruit that flows from the gift of God's Spirit in us. In Galatians, Paul writes:

So I say, let the Holy Spirit guide your lives. Then you won't be doing what your sinful nature craves. The sinful nature wants to do evil, which is just the opposite of what the Spirit wants. And the Spirit gives us desires that are the opposite of what the sinful nature desires. These two forces are constantly fighting each other, so you are not free to carry out your good intentions. But when you are directed by the Spirit, you are not under obligation to the law of Moses.

THE FRUIT OF THE SPIRIT

When you follow the desires of your sinful nature, the results are very clear: sexual immorality, impurity, lustful pleasures, idolatry, sorcery, hostility, quarrelling, jealousy, outbursts of anger, selfish ambition, dissension, division, envy, drunkenness, wild parties, and other sins like these. Let me tell you again, as I have before, that anyone living that sort of life will not inherit the Kingdom of God.

But the Holy Spirit produces this kind of fruit in our lives: love, joy, peace, patience, kindness, goodness, faithfulness, gentleness, and self-control. There is no law against these things!

Those who belong to Christ Jesus have nailed the passions and desires of their sinful nature to his cross and crucified them there. Since we are living by the Spirit, let us follow the Spirit's leading in every part of our lives. Let us not become conceited, or provoke one another, or be jealous of one another.

Galatians 5:16-26

As we explore each of the fruit of the Spirit – love, joy, peace, patience, kindness, goodness, faithfulness, gentleness and self-control – we take time to pause and listen to where God might be speaking to us. We open our hearts and our minds to Him and with prayerful anticipation, ask the Holy Spirit to guide our reflection.

A Prayer of Self-Offering

In this dry landscape,
I offer you, Lord Jesus,
the parched places of my life,
drained dry by others,
or long untended by my own wrong choices,
crusted with bitterness,
cracked by despair,
brittle and shrivelled,
bearing no good fruit.
As drenching rain and softening showers
bring new life to the bush,
forgive me and heal me, I pray,
with the grace that flows from your cross.
In this rich landscape,
I offer you, Lord Jesus,
the secret treasures of my life,
denied by others,
or dismissed by my own self-doubt,
dusty with neglect,
dormant or unnoticed,
packed with potential,
deeds of awakening life.
As ash after fire
nourishes the green shoots of regeneration,
give me the power of your resurrection, I pray,
with the Spirit you breathe on your friends.

— Elizabeth Smith [2]

LOVE

Life consists of three loves:
Love of God
Love of self
Love of others.

If we are to live fully:
If we are to grow toward wholeness;
If we are to feed the hungry hearts of others
Each love must be learned separately
Then carefully and patiently integrated.

— Betty W. Skinner, The Hidden Life (2006) [3]

We might say that we "love" pasta, or "love" clothes. We "love" TV shows and we "love" weekends. In our day and age, love is a word that seems to flow freely as a self-focused representation of our preferences and desires.

So, what distinguishes love through the Spirit, from the world's love? When love is expressed as a fruit of the Holy Spirit it glorifies God and draws people to Him.

As we seek to love God and to love our neighbours as ourselves, we are asked to step out from under the shadow of the shallow, self-serving love that the world would have us pursue. Instead, we humbly invite the Holy Spirit to empower us to live and love like Jesus.

PART 1: LOVE OF GOD

As you begin, take a moment to listen to the song "How Great is Your Love" by Phil Wickham.

We love each other because he loved us first.

1 John 4:19

For this is how God loved the world: He gave his one and only Son, so that everyone who believes in him will not perish but have eternal life.

John 3:16

Sit with these verses for a few minutes, then allow your heart and pen to speak out a prayer of thankfulness for God's gift of love to you. You are loved. How does it feel to hold these words in your heart? What does it mean to you to know that God sent Jesus to die for you? Do you have a visceral sense of God's love? Describe it.

Jesus' invitation to us, the same as God's invitation to His people in the Old Testament is to:

… love the Lord your God with all your heart, all your soul, all your strength, and all your mind …

Luke 10:27 and Deuteronomy 6

Spend some time reflecting on how you love God with each of these aspects of who you are (your heart, your soul, your strength, your mind). Which aspects come easily? Which aspects do you nurture? Which do you find more difficult? Are there any that you neglect? Invite God's Spirit to show you how to love Him more fully.

O Love, struggling to break through.
Why am I so blind to simple things?
The hush of Your Presence that the meadow brings
Are but fragments of infinite loving, never my own.
The depth of Your secrets are still hidden from view
Way beyond mountains, meadows and skies.
Please, Love, embrace me; open my eyes.
Burn in me brightly. Light the whole world.

— Betty W. Skinner, The Hidden Life (2006) [4]

ON RETREAT: EXPLORING THE FRUIT OF THE SPIRIT

LOVE

PART 2: LOVE OF SELF

As you begin, take a moment to listen to the song "How He Loves" by Dave Crowder Band.

You made all the delicate, inner parts of my body
 and knit me together in my mother's womb.
Thank you for making me so wonderfully complex!
 Your workmanship is marvelous—how well I know it.
You watched me as I was being formed in utter seclusion,
 as I was woven together in the dark of the womb.
You saw me before I was born.
 Every day of my life was recorded in your book.
Every moment was laid out
 before a single day had passed.

How precious are your thoughts about me, O God.
 They cannot be numbered!
I can't even count them;
 they outnumber the grains of sand!
And when I wake up,
 you are still with me!

Psalm 139:13-18

God wants you to see yourself as he sees you - utterly loved – and to love yourself as you fulfill His request to love others. Loving yourself can sometimes feel like it's out of balance with God's other instructions.

Do not think of yourself more highly than you ought, but rather think of yourself with sober judgment, in accordance with the faith God has distributed to each of you.

Romans 12:3 (NIV)

LOVE

This "sober judgement" is advice meant to balance out the extremes that we might otherwise experience – "more highly than you ought", but also more lowly than is Godly. An ever-adjusting equilibrium of repentance and awareness of being "made in His image".

Repentance shouldn't be self-flagellation or excessive criticism but turning to Jesus with a deep desire for Him to develop the opposite quality in you. When looking at your sins through the lens of Jesus' cross and resurrection, there is the opportunity for the potential opposite quality to emerge. For example, when you see selfishness, don't be discouraged, but rejoice that your real quality – the opposite of selfishness, love – wants to emerge. It is about cooperating with Jesus as He creates in you a new heart that can love and live the way you were meant to.

A picture to ponder:
Stripped naked,
then re-clothed
with the most beautiful, soft white linen robe
of righteousness
and peace
and companionship. [5]

Can you let your imagination picture this? How does it look? How does it feel?

Take some time to sit with the passage from Psalm 139. Give yourself permission to look at yourself through the eyes of God. What do you see? What is different to what you usually see? What do you struggle to "love" in yourself? What is the mirror image opposite quality that Jesus wants to emerge as you cooperate with Him?

"You have to listen to the voice who calls you the beloved, because otherwise you will run around begging for affirmation, for praise, for success."

— *Henri Nouwen* [6]

LOVE

ON RETREAT: EXPLORING THE FRUIT OF THE SPIRIT

PART 3: LOVE OF OTHERS

As you begin, take a moment to listen to the song "The Proof of Your Love" by for KING & COUNTRY.

During this session, use the practice of Lectio Divina (described on page 161) to prayerfully reflect on the following passage of scripture:

Dear friends, let us continue to love one another, for love comes from God. Anyone who loves is a child of God and knows God. But anyone who does not love does not know God, for God is love.

God showed how much he loved us by sending his one and only Son into the world so that we might have eternal life through him. This is real love—not that we loved God, but that he loved us and sent his Son as a sacrifice to take away our sins.

Dear friends, since God loved us that much, we surely ought to love each other. No one has ever seen God. But if we love each other, God lives in us, and his love is brought to full expression in us.

And God has given us his Spirit as proof that we live in him and he in us. Furthermore, we have seen with our own eyes and now testify that the Father sent his Son to be the Savior of the world. All who declare that Jesus is the Son of God have God living in them, and they live in God. We know how much God loves us, and we have put our trust in his love.

God is love, and all who live in love live in God, and God lives in them. And as we live in God, our love grows more perfect. So we will not be afraid on the day of judgment, but we can face him with confidence because we live like Jesus here in this world.

Such love has no fear, because perfect love expels all fear. If we are afraid, it is for fear of punishment, and this shows that we have not fully experienced his perfect love. We love each other because he loved us first.

If someone says, "I love God," but hates a fellow believer, that person is a liar; for if we don't love people we can see, how can we love God, whom we cannot see?

1 John 4:7-20

What does it mean to you to know that God sent Jesus to die for those around you?

Does the knowledge that we each have the Spirit of God living within us shape the way you think of others?

How can you allow God's love for you to expand - to touch the lives of those around you?

Of all God's gifts, love excels
It is larger,
It is stronger,
It is fuller,
It is higher,
It is more joyful,
It is more beautiful,
Nothing in all of earth
Nor anything in heaven is better,
For Love is truly God
And God is Love!

— Betty W. Skinner, The Circle of Love (2006) [7]

ON RETREAT: EXPLORING THE FRUIT OF THE SPIRIT

LOVE

JOY

*With joy you will drink deeply
 from the fountain of salvation!
In that wonderful day you will sing:
 "Thank the Lord! Praise his name!
Tell the nations what he has done.
 Let them know how mighty he is!"*

Isaiah 12:3-4

That wonderful day speaks of Jesus - of the joy and freedom that comes from our salvation. A celebration of the grace that we have been shown by God.

Some questions to ponder: Does the joy of your salvation resonate in your heart? Do you draw joy from your spiritual journey? From the twists and turns of life? Do you draw joy from God's constant presence with you? Do you look to the future with joy and hopeful anticipation of how God will move in your life? Do you share the joy of your salvation with others?

For Christians, joy has a broader and much deeper meaning than happiness. Joy is about celebrating the gifts God has given us, despite our circumstances, despite how we might feel, despite our fears and failings. Joy is about opening our hearts to Him with gratitude, for the gift of our salvation.

PART 1: JOY FOR THE PAST

As you begin, take a moment to listen to the song "Where I'm Standing Now" by Phil Wickham.

To illustrate the point further, Jesus told them this story: "A man had two sons. The younger son told his father, 'I want my share of your estate now before you die.' So his father agreed to divide his wealth between his sons.

"A few days later this younger son packed all his belongings and moved to a distant land, and there he wasted all his money in wild living. About the time his money ran out, a great famine swept over the land, and he began to starve. He persuaded a local farmer to hire him, and the man sent him into his fields to feed the pigs. The young man became so hungry that even the pods he was feeding the pigs looked good to him. But no one gave him anything.

"When he finally came to his senses, he said to himself, 'At home even the hired servants have food enough to spare, and here I am dying of hunger! I will go home to my father and say, "Father, I have sinned against both heaven and you, and I am no longer worthy of being called your son. Please take me on as a hired servant."'

"So he returned home to his father. And while he was still a long way off, his father saw him coming. Filled with love and compassion, he ran to his son, embraced him, and kissed him. His son said to him, 'Father, I have sinned against both heaven and you, and I am no longer worthy of being called your son.'

"But his father said to the servants, 'Quick! Bring the finest robe in the house and put it on him. Get a ring for his finger and sandals for his feet. And kill the calf we have been fattening. We must celebrate with a feast, for this son of mine was dead and has now returned to life. He was lost, but now he is found.' So the party began.

"Meanwhile, the older son was in the fields working. When he returned home, he heard music and dancing in the house, and he asked one of the servants what was going on. 'Your brother is back,' he was told, 'and your father has killed the fattened calf. We are celebrating because of his safe return.'

"The older brother was angry and wouldn't go in. His father came out and begged him, but he replied, 'All these years I've slaved for you and never once refused to do a single thing you told me to. And in all that time you never gave me even one young goat for a feast with my friends. Yet when this son of yours comes back after squandering your money on prostitutes, you celebrate by killing the fattened calf!'

"His father said to him, 'Look, dear son, you have always stayed by me, and everything I have is yours. We had to celebrate this happy day. For your brother was dead and has come back to life! He was lost, but now he is found!'"

Luke 15:11-32

How did the prodigal son retell this story? How might he have shared it with his friends, his children and grandchildren? Was there joy as he shared about the gift of unexpected forgiveness when he returned home from his wayward journey?

How did the older brother retell this story? How did he describe the return of his brother and their father's reaction? Did he live with anger and resentment his whole life? Or was his heart eventually changed?

How did the father retell this story? Did his heart struggle with the juxtaposition that he faced - answered prayer and a younger son returned to him, yet an older son still "lost" in his own way? Did the father remain joyful considering his disappointment? Or did his disappointment gradually rob him of that joy?

We are going to apply the principles of the Prayer of Examen (described on page 163), but instead of looking at a day, we will look back over our whole life journey.

Find a comfortable position. Take some time to relax, and become still, in body, mind and spirit. Take some slow, regular breaths reminded of God's presence through the Holy Spirit.

Ask God to bring to your awareness the events of your life that He wants you to notice. Gently play back, from primary school to high school, to your journey into adulthood. Just as you would press the pause button on a movie, linger on the people, places and happenings that catch your attention. Let them touch you again as you remember them. You may be surprised by what you notice - fear, anger, hurt, disgust, sadness, happiness, confidence, pride, contentment. As you re-experience your life and as people, places and events come to mind, ask God what He is saying to you through this awareness. Be open to His leading.

As you reflect, are there pieces of your story that linger - fuelling patterns of bitterness and resentment within you? Does holding onto those moments rob you of joy today? Can you celebrate the fact that God has brought you through this part of your story?

Are there pieces of your story that have become a source of joy for you? Moments of growth or redemption? Do you celebrate these stories? Do you share them as an offering of hope to the people around you?

Have there been moments in your life where you can relate to the prodigal son, the older brother, or the father? As you recognise this, can you imagine Jesus sharing your story as a parable? What might he say?

Respond spontaneously and truthfully from your heart – with joy, gratitude, sadness, a cry for help, or perhaps a prayer of deepening trust – whatever is authentic for you.

"Celebration belongs to God's Kingdom. God not only offers forgiveness, reconciliation, and healing, but wants to lift up these gifts as a source of joy for all who witness them. In all three of the parables which Jesus tells to explain why he eats with sinners; God rejoices and invites others to rejoice with him. "Rejoice with me," the shepherd says, "I have found my sheep that was lost." "Rejoice with me," the woman says, "I have found the drachma I lost." "Rejoice with me," the father says, "this son of mine was lost and is found." All these voices are the voices of God. God does not want to keep his joy to himself. He wants everyone to share in it. God's joy is the joy of his angels and his saints; it is the joy of all who belong to the Kingdom."

— Henri Nouwen, The Return of the Prodigal Son *(1994)* [8]

ON RETREAT: EXPLORING THE FRUIT OF THE SPIRIT

JOY

PART 2: JOY IN THE PRESENT

As you begin, take a moment to listen to the song "The Joy" by The Belonging Co.

The one I love calls to me:
Arise, my dearest. Hurry, my darling.
  Come away with me!
  I have come as you have asked
  to draw you to my heart and lead you out.
  For now is the time, my beautiful one.
The season has changed,
  the bondage of your barren winter has ended,
  and the season of hiding is over and gone.
  The rains have soaked the earth
and left it bright with blossoming flowers.
  The season for singing and pruning the vines has arrived.
  I hear the cooing of doves in our land,
  filling the air with songs to awaken you and guide you forth.

Can you not discern this new day of destiny breaking forth around you?
  The early signs of my purposes and plans
  are bursting forth.
  The budding vines of new life
  are now blooming everywhere.
  The fragrance of their flowers whispers,
  "There is change in the air."
  Arise, my love, my beautiful companion,
  and run with me to the higher place.
  For now is the time to arise and come away with me.
For you are my dove, hidden in the split-open rock.
  It was I who took you and hid you up high
  in the secret stairway of the sky.

Let me see your radiant face and hear your sweet voice.
How beautiful your eyes of worship
and lovely your voice in prayer.

You must catch the troubling foxes, those sly little foxes that hinder our relationship.

For they raid our budding vineyard of love to ruin what I've planted within you. Will you catch them and remove them for me? We will do it together.

Song of Songs 2:10-15 (TPT)

In this passage, the Shephard-King calls to the Shulamite:
- inviting her to a new season (v11-12)
- inviting her to a new life (v13)
- reminding her that she is precious (v14)
- reminding her that she is not alone (v15)

Written by King Solomon, Song of Songs has been interpreted in many ways over centuries past – as a love story between a man and a woman, as a literal encounter between Solomon and a Shulamite woman, as a dream, as an allegory and more.

Read the passage again slowly, pausing after every few lines, and this time, consider it as a deeply symbolic representation of Christ and the church - as a melody sung from the heart of Jesus for you, his longing bride.

As you read, can you hear Jesus calling you to "come away" with Him? Can you hear Jesus' invitation to your heart - to bask in the joy of your salvation, to embrace the new life He offers you afresh, every day? How does it feel to be free from "bondage" and "hiding"? Can you see yourself with His eyes? What are the "blossoming flowers", "budding vines", "fragrant flowers" in your life right now? Where might He be inviting you to grow?

Can you hear His voice of love which sets you apart as His precious one? How does it feel to know that you are protected by Him? Can you hear Jesus speaking words of love over you? "My dove" ... "radiant" ... "beautiful" ... "lovely" ...

Can you hear the promise of His constant presence? His assurance that He is with you now and forevermore? What are the "troubling foxes" that threaten your "budding vineyard of love"? Do they rob you of the joy of what has been "planted within you"? How does it feel to know that He will help you to remove the foxes?

How might this passage help you to reframe the aspects of your life where you currently feel consumed or stuck?

*Help me to remember, Father,
that this time of joy
will never come again.
Let me savour the fullness of it.
Let me share the beauty of it
that others might feel
and know it too.*

— Betty W. Skinner, The Hidden Life (2006) [9]

ON RETREAT: EXPLORING THE FRUIT OF THE SPIRIT

JOY

PART 3: JOY FOR THE FUTURE

As you begin, take a moment to listen to the song "Joy" by Rend Collective.

Joy is a theme that weaves its way throughout the Bible. God expressed joy as he saw that the world that He created was good (Genesis 1). There are proverbs that describe children (Proverbs 23:24-25) and friends (Proverbs 27:9) as a source of joy. The angels rejoiced with the birth of the Messiah (Luke 2:10). Jesus expressed joy and thanksgiving as he prayed to God (Luke 10:21). There are also stories of joy, woven within times of struggle:

The Israelites rejoiced as they left Egypt, even as they headed into the desert.

So he brought his people out of Egypt with joy,

his chosen ones with rejoicing.

Psalm 105:43

The prophet Isaiah spoke of the rejoicing that would come at the end of the Babylonian oppression.

Those who have been ransomed by the Lord will return.

They will enter Jerusalem singing,

crowned with everlasting joy.

Sorrow and mourning will disappear,

and they will be filled with joy and gladness.

Isaiah 51:11

Paul and Barnabas were filled with joy despite being run out of Antioch.

Then the Jews stirred up the influential religious women and the leaders of the city, and they incited a mob against Paul and Barnabas and ran them out of town. So they shook the dust from their feet as a sign of rejection and went to the town of Iconium. And the believers were filled with joy and with the Holy Spirit.

Acts 13:50-52

Paul spoke of his joy for life, despite being in prison.

For to me, living means living for Christ, and dying is even better. But if I live, I can do more fruitful work for Christ. So I really don't know which is better. I'm torn between two desires: I long to go and be with Christ, which would be far better for me. But for your sakes, it is better that I continue to live. Knowing this, I am convinced that I will remain alive so I can continue to help all of you grow and experience the joy of your faith.

Philippians 1:21-25

For the Israelites, for Isaiah, for Paul and for Barnabas, joy was about celebrating the gifts that God had given them despite their circumstances, despite how they felt and despite their fears. And it can be the same for us.

Joy is an attitude that we adopt - not because of our circumstances, but because of our hope in God's love and promise. Joy is about opening our hearts to God with gratitude for the gift of our salvation. Joy is not determined by our struggles, but our future destiny.

Let's reflect on the joy that flows from the confidence of our salvation using the practice of Lectio Divina (described on page 161) and the following passage of scripture:

All praise to God, the Father of our Lord Jesus Christ. It is by his great mercy that we have been born again, because God raised Jesus Christ from the dead. Now we live with great expectation, and we have a priceless inheritance—an inheritance that is kept in heaven for you, pure and undefiled, beyond the reach of change and decay. And through your faith, God is protecting you by his power until you receive this salvation, which is ready to be revealed on the last day for all to see.

So be truly glad. There is wonderful joy ahead, even though you must endure many trials for a little while. These trials will show that your faith is genuine. It is being tested as fire tests and purifies gold— though your faith is far more precious than mere gold. So when your faith remains strong through many trials, it will bring you much praise and glory and honor on the day when Jesus Christ is revealed to the whole world.

You love him even though you have never seen him. Though you do not see him now, you trust him; and you rejoice with a glorious, inexpressible joy. The reward for trusting him will be the salvation of your souls.

1 Peter 1:3-9

Do you look to the future with joy and hopeful anticipation of how God will move in your life?

Do you rejoice in your salvation? How do you outwardly express this joy? How do you express this joy with others? How do you express this joy to God?

Can you recall a time of spiritual celebration? Allow yourself to experience that joy again.

Waken in Me a Sense of Joy

O extravagant God,
in this ripening, red-tinged autumn,
waken in me a sense of joy
    in just being alive,
joy for nothing in general
    except everything in particular;
joy in sun and rain
    mating with earth to birth a harvest;
joy in soft light
    through shyly disrobing trees;
joy in acolyte moon
    setting halos around processing clouds;
joy in the beating of a thousand wings
    mysteriously knowing which way is warm;
joy in wagging tails and kids' smiles
    and in this spunky old city;
joy in the taste of bread and wine,
    the smell of dawn,
        a touch,
            a song,
                a presence;
joy in having what I cannot live without —
    other people to hold and cry and laugh with;
joy in love,
    in you;
and that all at first and last
    is grace.

— Ted Loder, *Guerillas of Grace* (1981) [10]

ON RETREAT: EXPLORING THE FRUIT OF THE SPIRIT

JOY

PEACE

Peace is belief that exhales. Because you believe that God's provision is everywhere - like air.

— Ann Voskamp, The Greatest Gift: Unwrapping the Full Love Story of Christmas (2013) [11]

Biblical peace means more than simply being at rest, still or quiet, or living a life without conflict. It is not just a state of inner tranquillity, but a state of wholeness and completeness. We can't create peace on our own. This fruit of the Spirit flows from the deep confidence that our lives are in the hands of a loving and compassionate God.

As you begin, take a moment to listen to the song "Peace" by Bethel Music.

PART 1: PEACE COMES FROM GOD

Peace is a fruit of the Spirit. In John 14:1-20 we read of the Spirit, the advocate, that Jesus promises to send His disciples when He leaves the earth. Jesus speaks these words down through the centuries also to us. This Spirit will help you love God and give you wisdom and peace.

During this session, use the practice of Lectio Divina (described on page 161) to prayerfully reflect on the following passage of scripture:

"Don't let your hearts be troubled. Trust in God, and trust also in me. There is more than enough room in my Father's home. If this were not so, would I have told you that I am going to prepare a place for you? When everything is ready, I will come and get you, so that you will always be with me where I am. And you know the way to where I am going."

"No, we don't know, Lord," Thomas said. "We have no idea where you are going, so how can we know the way?"

Jesus told him, "I am the way, the truth, and the life. No one can come to the Father except through me. If you had really known me, you would know who my Father is. From now on, you do know him and have seen him!"

Philip said, "Lord, show us the Father, and we will be satisfied."

Jesus replied, "Have I been with you all this time, Philip, and yet you still don't know who I am? Anyone who has seen me has seen the Father! So why are you asking me to show him to you? Don't you believe that I am in the Father and the Father is in me? The words I speak are not my own, but my Father who lives in me does his work through me. Just believe that I am in the Father and the Father is in me. Or at least believe because of the work you have seen me do.

"I tell you the truth, anyone who believes in me will do the same works I have done, and even greater works, because I am going to be with the Father. You can ask for anything in my name, and I will do it, so that the Son can bring glory to the Father. Yes, ask me for anything in my name, and I will do it!

"If you love me, obey my commandments. And I will ask the Father, and he will give you another Advocate, who will never leave you. He is the Holy Spirit, who leads into all truth. The world cannot receive him, because it isn't looking for him and doesn't recognize him. But you know him, because he lives with you now and later will be in you. No, I will not abandon you as orphans—I will come to you. Soon the world will no longer see me, but you will see me. Since I live, you also will live. When I am raised to life again, you will know that I am in my Father, and you are in me, and I am in you.

John 14:1-20

What troubles your heart?

Where do you need the Spirit's help?

PEACE

ON RETREAT: EXPLORING THE FRUIT OF THE SPIRIT

PART 2: PEACE IS A PROTECTION

As you begin, take a moment to listen to the song "Still / PEACE" by Hillsong Worship.

Do not be anxious about anything, but in every situation, by prayer and petition, with thanksgiving, present your requests to God. And the peace of God, which transcends all understanding, will guard your hearts and your minds in Christ Jesus.

Philippians 4:6-7

Can you think of some sports where a guard is worn?
hockey: mouth guard
cricket: crotch guard
ice hockey: helmet (head guard)

"… the peace of God … will guard your hearts and minds"

Here Paul describes the Spirit's gift of peace as a "protection". Have you ever thought of wearing the Spirit's peace as a mind and heart guard? What would you imagine it looks like?

"Breastplate of righteousness" (Ephesians 6:14b)
"Helmet of salvation" (Ephesians 6:17)

The physical representations of the heart in the chest and mind in the head, are given "protections" in Ephesians 6. The "protections" are about knowing and believing where you stand in Jesus.

This "protection of peace" in Philippians is described to be specifically against the onslaught of anxiety. What are triggers for anxiety, or anxious thoughts for you? Are you aware of any anxious thoughts, right now, sitting at the edges of your mind? Can you list them all?

Ann Voskamp says that "Worry is belief gone wrong. Because you don't believe that God will get it right".[12]

This "protection of peace" comes, as you pray. "But in every situation, by prayer and petition, with thanksgiving, present your requests to God".

The "protection of peace" comes as you talk with God in "every situation". Filled with thanksgiving for the intimate relationship you have with God, you talk about your concerns and heaviness and anxieties; you bring them to God.

Would you like to bring that list of anxious thoughts to God right now?

This "protection of peace" is not just any peace - it's Divine peace that "transcends all understanding."

What is your "thankful" response, knowing the Mighty Creator God, your Saviour and friend, wants you to bring these things to Him?

Empty Me

Gracious and Holy One,
    creator of all things
        and of emptiness,
I come to you
    full of much that clutters and distracts,
        stifles and burdens me,
            and makes me a burden to others.
Empty me now
    of gnawing dissatisfactions,
        of anxious imaginings
            of fretful preoccupations,
    of nagging prejudices,
        of old scores to settle,
            and of the arrogance of being right.
Empty me
    of the ways I unthinkingly think of myself as powerless,
        as a victim,
            as determined by sex, age, race,
            as being less than I am,
                or as other than yours.
Empty me
    of the disguises and lies
        in which I hide myself from other people
        and from my responsibility
            for my neighbors and for the world.

Hollow out in me a space
   in which I will find myself,
      find peace and a whole heart,
         a forgiving spirit and holiness,
           the springs of laughter,
      and the will to reach boldly
         for abundant life for myself
           and the whole human family.

— Ted Loder, *Guerillas of Grace* (1981) [13]

PEACE

ON RETREAT: EXPLORING THE FRUIT OF THE SPIRIT

PART 3: PEACE IS AN ACTION

As you begin, take a moment to listen to the song "Peace" by Hillsong Young & Free.

Peace is an active decision - a choice as well as a gift to receive. Jesus gifts peace to us through His Spirit, then He wants us to reciprocally gift peace to others.

"Seek peace and pursue it."

1 Peter 3:11

"Let peace rule in your hearts."

Colossians 3:15

"Keep unity through peace."

Ephesians 4:13

The prophet Daniel was a young, Jewish noble who was rounded up with all of God's people and taken to be exiled under Nebuchadnezzar, king of Babylon. From the captives, Daniel and three of his friends were selected to be trained in the language and culture of the Babylonians because of their looks and intelligence. In many ways, Daniel demonstrates an "actioning" of peace in his life and choices. Read through chapters 1, 2 and 4 of the book of Daniel and list the ways you can identify Daniel living out peace.

Can you think of ways you have "actioned" peace in your own life?

Are there spaces in your life right now where God might be inviting you to "action" peace?

Draw me to Yourself

In this moment
draw me to yourself, Lord,
and make me aware
    not so much of what I've given
        as of all I have received
            and so have yet to share.
Send me forth
    in power and gladness
        and with great courage
            to live out in the world
                what I pray and profess,
that, in sharing,
    I may do justice,
        make peace,
           grow in love,
                enjoy myself,
                    other people,
                      and your world now,
                      and you forever.

— Ted Loder, *Guerillas of Grace (1981)* [14]

PEACE

ON RETREAT: EXPLORING THE FRUIT OF THE SPIRIT

PATIENCE

"So here's what I want you to do, God helping you: Take your everyday, ordinary life - your sleeping, eating, going-to-work, and walking-around life - and place it before God as an offering. Embracing what God does for you is the best thing you can do for him. Don't become so well-adjusted to your culture that you fit into it without even thinking. Instead, fix your attention on God. You'll be changed from the inside out. Readily recognize what he wants from you, and quickly respond to it. Unlike the culture around you, always dragging you down to its level of immaturity, God brings the best out of you, develops well-formed maturity in you."

Romans 12:1-2 (MSG)

Patience is counter cultural – it's something that slows us down, it interrupts our productivity, and it doesn't yield immediate results.

In Romans, Paul encourages the early church to set themselves apart from the culture of the day. He implores them to fix their attention on God so that they might be changed from the inside out, rather than allow themselves to settle into the patterns of the world around them.

While our culture of instant gratification and hurry would have us move in one direction, God calls us to move in an opposite direction - to grow in patience with the help of the Holy Spirit, to live in the present moment, to wait with grace, to be patient with ourselves and with others, and to trust God's unhurried plan for our lives.

PART 1: PATIENCE IN WAITING

As you begin, take a moment to listen to the song "Patient" by Apollo Ltd.

Waiting is not just a patient act.
Waiting is a way of living.
We learn it as we grow in God.
To learn to wait with Him is difficult.
To wait with Him expectantly is an accomplishment.
To wait with Him in peace is victorious.

— Betty W. Skinner, The Circle of Love (2006) [15]

We're not used to waiting. Takeaway food shortcuts the need for preparation and cooking in the kitchen. Why would you layby when you can Afterpay or Zip Pay and take your items now? We email and text in preference to snail mail or phone calls and hook up culture sees people skipping courtship and fast forwarding to intimacy.

Sometimes waiting is an unavoidable part of life – when we're pregnant, when we're studying, when we're growing up! Oftentimes waiting is frustrating and we wonder why we must go through it – when we're recovering from injury, when we feel stuck in a situation, when God doesn't seem to be moving the way we'd hoped.

Waiting is a part of life that we seem to have forgotten, but one that God gifts us with as a mechanism to grow our patience, trust and dependence on Him.

In Jeremiah, we read of God's promise to the exiles of Babylon.

Captured and carried away as prisoners of King Nebuchadnezzar, they were far from their "promised land" and far from freedom. But despite their captivity, God asks them to settle in, and to wait! Not to mourn what they had lost, but to flourish in this foreign setting. To flourish in the waiting. Then He reassures them that this waiting is for their good.

This is what the Lord of Heaven's Armies, the God of Israel, says to all the captives he has exiled to Babylon from Jerusalem: "Build homes, and plan to stay. Plant gardens, and eat the food they produce. Marry and have children. Then find spouses for them so that you may have many grandchildren. Multiply! Do not dwindle away! And work for the peace and prosperity of the city where I sent you into exile. Pray to the Lord for it, for its welfare will determine your welfare."

This is what the Lord of Heaven's Armies, the God of Israel, says: "Do not let your prophets and fortune-tellers who are with you in the land of Babylon trick you. Do not listen to their dreams, because they are telling you lies in my name. I have not sent them," says the Lord.

This is what the Lord says: "You will be in Babylon for seventy years. But then I will come and do for you all the good things I have promised, and I will bring you home again. For I know the plans I have for you," says the Lord. "They are plans for good and not for disaster, to give you a future and a hope. In those days when you pray, I will listen. If you look for me wholeheartedly, you will find me. I will be found by you," says the Lord. "I will end your captivity and restore your fortunes. I will gather you out of the nations where I sent you and will bring you home again to your own land."

Jeremiah 29:4-14

Can you recall a period of "waiting" that you have journeyed through in your life? How did you respond as you waited? What feelings were you aware of? Allow yourself to feel them again. As you sit with your feelings, notice where in your body they resonate (If you remember anxiety, then maybe your chest feels tight or your gut clenches. If you felt fear, then maybe your heart races in response). What might God be wanting to show you in this felt experience?

As you reflect on your "waiting", are you aware of any growth in you during this time? You may not know why you were called to wait, but can you see any fruit from that period? Ask God to show you. What might God be inviting you to notice, as you reflect on the "waiting" you've done in the past?

Is there something that you're "waiting" through now? Can you wait with anticipation for what this period might bring? Can you be present to each moment of your "waiting" instead of seeking to hurry through it?

Grant Me Your Sense of Timing

O God of all seasons and senses,
grant me your sense of timing
   to submit gracefully
      and rejoice quietly
         in the turn of the seasons.

In this season of short days and long nights,
   of grey and white and cold,
teach me the lessons of waiting:
   of the snow joining the mystery
     of the hunkered-down seeds
       growing in their sleep
         watched over by gnarled-limbed, grandparent trees
           resting from autumn's staggering energy;
        of the silent, whirling earth
           circling to race back home to the sun.
O God, grant me your sense of timing.

In this season of short days and long nights,
   of grey and white and cold,
teach me the lessons of endings:
   children growing, friends leaving,
     jobs concluding,
       stages finishing,
         grieving over,
           grudges over,
             blaming over,
               excuses over.
O God, grant me your sense of timing.

In this season of short days and long nights,
 of grey and white and cold,
teach me the lessons of beginnings:
 that such waitings and endings
  may be a starting place,
   a of planting seeds
    which bring to birth
     what is ready to be born -
      something right and just and different,
       a new song,
        a deeper relationship,
         a fuller love -
          in the fullness of your time.
O God, grant me your sense of timing.

— Ted Loder, *Guerillas of Grace (1981)* [16]

PATIENCE

ON RETREAT: EXPLORING THE FRUIT OF THE SPIRIT

PART 2: PATIENCE IN OUR FAILING

As you begin, take a moment to listen to the song "Graves into Gardens" by Koryn Hawthorn.

Are there patterns and behaviours that you notice within yourself, that come up time and time again? Sometimes God reveals something to us and we think we have it mastered, only to have the same heart issue pop up a little while later, just in a slightly different way. We work through that scenario, but then another variation of the same underlying issue comes up and then another and another.

It can feel like we're making no progress at all, like we're playing "whack-a-mole" or trying to cut down a tree, one leaf at a time. It can be a frustrating process - a painful process.

Sin is unfortunately, a fundamental component of our humanity. In Romans 3 Paul writes "For everyone has sinned; we all fall short of God's glorious standard". Sometimes the patterns of our sinful behaviour run deep. But Paul also reminds us that "God, in his grace, freely makes us right in his sight. He did this through Christ Jesus when he freed us from the penalty for our sins". We are sinful by nature and yet we are redeemed by a loving God who extends patience and grace to us despite our failings.

What I don't understand about myself is that I decide one way, but then I act another, doing things I absolutely despise. So if I can't be trusted to figure out what is best for myself and then do it, it becomes obvious that God's command is necessary.

But I need something more! For if I know the law but still can't keep it, and if the power of sin within me keeps sabotaging my best intentions, I obviously need help! I realize that I don't have what it takes. I can will it, but I can't do it. I decide to do good, but I don't really do it; I decide not to do bad, but then I do it anyway. My decisions, such as they are, don't result in actions. Something has gone wrong deep within me and gets the better of me every time.

It happens so regularly that it's predictable. The moment I decide to do good, sin is there to trip me up. I truly delight in God's commands, but it's pretty obvious that not all of me joins in that delight. Parts of me covertly rebel, and just when I least expect it, they take charge.

I've tried everything and nothing helps. I'm at the end of my rope. Is there no one who can do anything for me? Isn't that the real question?

The answer, thank God, is that Jesus Christ can and does. He acted to set things right in this life of contradictions where I want to serve God with all my heart and mind, but am pulled by the influence of sin to do something totally different.

Romans 7:15-25 (MSG)

As you sit quietly with God, invite Him to show you where He has been patient with you in your journey.

Are there themes or recurring patterns of behaviour that you feel like you work through repeatedly? You might like to write about them in your journal. How does it feel to face your sin over and over again? Frustrating? Burdensome? Painful? Tiring? Hopeless? How has this area of sin impacted your self-image? Your relationship with God? Your relationship with others?

God is gracious and patient with us. He knows that we will sin and yet He loves us anyway. Have you allowed yourself to experience His grace in this journey? Can you be patient with yourself each time you work through a pattern of sin, just as God is patient with you? Can you allow the patience that God has shown you to flow into your relationships with others? Can you be patient with others who stumble? Do you show grace to others who fall?

The Saving I Need

I used to cry out to you
For you
With fervour and volume
Not ceasing to bid
For divine intervention
Asking you to come
Like a rider of clouds
Like Deus Ex Machina
Like a warrior king

I'd petition you
To deliver me
And save me
From my suffering
From my lack
From my angst
And you did
You did
Till you didn't

It's like you stopped
Stopped allowing
Me to see you that way
Far away
Worlds away
Pushed away
So you delivered me
You saved me

Saved me from the lie
That you were distant
That you could leave me
Forsake me
Go against your word
Your nature
And be anywhere other
Than with me
Be anyone other
Than Immanuel

So I quit working
Quit striving
Allowing myself to rest
I took a break
From burnt offerings
Burning myself
Beating myself
And started loving myself
Like you do
I started learning
What it meant to be me
With you by my side
And it was great
Really great
Till it wasn't
And I needed saving again

— David Tensen, *The Saving I Need* (2021) [17]

PATIENCE

PART 3: PATIENCE IN OUR RELATIONSHIPS

As you begin, take a moment to listen to the song "Patient Work" by Vineyard Worship.

Real, authentic love is what each of us deeply desires within our relationships. We want to experience agape love - a selfless love that is passionately committed to the well-being of others - the kind of love that focuses on what's important and releases what is trivial. But too often, our relationships are influenced by offence and in such circumstances, we respond by lashing out, withdrawing, avoiding, holding a grudge or becoming passive aggressive.

In 1 Corinthians 13, Paul describes love (as it applies in relationships) as patient. The Greek word for patience is *makrothymeō* which is the concatenation of two other Greek words – *makros* and *thymos*.

makros	big, broad, spread out, long
thymos	passion
makrothymeō	"stretched out passion", long-suffering, perseverance

In our relationships, we are called to love with patience. We are asked to be longsuffering in the face of tough circumstances, to allow our passion for the other to stretch beyond the hurt. Patience asks us to bear the offence quietly rather than respond rashly.

In our individualistic culture, the concept of being long-suffering in our relationships goes against the norm. Our Western value system encourages people to do what makes them happy and to look out for number one. But God calls us to stand with the other person when we are offended, not to retaliate or put our own needs above theirs. He asks us to demonstrate patience repeatedly - to be long-suffering, to stand by the other despite our hurt.

Of course, though, demonstrating patience and an attitude of long suffering is not God's invitation in any relationship where there is a distortion of power leading to abuse. Abuse comes from an attitude of control and blatant disrespect for the value of another human. In a relationship where there is any form of abuse (physical or emotional), there is a higher standard of setting boundaries for the safety and protection of the individual. Patience is never an excuse for the tolerance of abuse. Patience is a choice made, recognising the value of each person and the importance of extending grace to encourage the healthy growth of the relationship.

Let's reflect on the concept of long-suffering using the method of Lectio Divina (described on page 161) and the following passages:

Not only so, but we also glory in our sufferings, because we know that suffering produces perseverance; perseverance, character; and character, hope. And hope does not put us to shame, because God's love has been poured out into our hearts through the Holy Spirit, who has been given to us.

Romans 5:3-5

Always be humble and gentle. Be patient with each other, making allowance for each other's faults because of your love.

Ephesians 4:2

Be assured that from the first day we heard of you, we haven't stopped praying for you, asking God to give you wise minds and spirits attuned to his will, and so acquire a thorough understanding of the ways in which God works. We pray that you'll live well for the Master, making him proud of you as you work hard in his orchard. As you learn more and more how God works, you will learn how to do your work. We pray that you'll have the strength to stick it out over the long haul—not the grim strength of gritting your teeth but the glory-strength God gives. It is strength that endures the unendurable and spills over into joy, thanking the Father who makes us strong enough to take part in everything bright and beautiful that he has for us.

Colossians 1:9-12 (MSG)

When have you suffered offence in a relationship? How did you respond?

When might you have been (or seen) long-suffering in a relationship?

What feelings do you notice rise in you, as you reflect? Allow yourself to feel them. Explore them. Notice where they sit within your body.

ON RETREAT: EXPLORING THE FRUIT OF THE SPIRIT

PATIENCE

KINDNESS

"Be the living expression of God's kindness: kindness in your face, kindness in your eyes, kindness in your smile."

— *Mother Teresa (1910 – 1997)*

Kindness is not just about having nice manners or being polite to the people around us. It flows from a heart posture which acknowledges each person as uniquely made in God's image and sees them as His beloved.

The Greek work for kindness is *chréstotés*. The closest translation of this word is "useful", which implies that kindness also involves action. Kindness is a fruit that we must step into and the more we actively pursue it, the more it outflows from our lives.

PART 1: A GIFT FROM GOD

As you begin, take a moment to listen to the song "Communion" by Brooke Ligertwood.

Let's explore kindness in God first, using the method of Lectio Divina (described on page 161) and the following passage:

Once we, too, were foolish and disobedient. We were misled and became slaves to many lusts and pleasures. Our lives were full of evil and envy, and we hated each other. But - when God our Savior revealed his kindness and love, he saved us, not because of the righteous things we had done, but because of his mercy. He washed away our sins, giving us a new birth and new life through the Holy Spirit. He generously poured out the Spirit upon us through Jesus Christ our Savior. Because of his grace he made us right in his sight and gave us confidence that we will inherit eternal life.

This is a trustworthy saying, and I want you to insist on these teachings so that all who trust in God will devote themselves to doing good. These teachings are good and beneficial for everyone.

Titus 3:3-8

How do you experience God's kindness in these verses? What does this kindness feel like? Does seeing your salvation as kindness bring a new awareness?

The Words in Red Matter

What if we
gave weight
to the words
in red. Saw the
text within the
context of love
and kindness.
Used the example
of how Christ
treated others as
confirmation
that a loving
God will
never turn anyone away.

— *Franki, How to Find Love in the Dark (2021)* [18]

KINDNESS

ON RETREAT: EXPLORING THE FRUIT OF THE SPIRIT

PART 2: A POSTURE OF THE HEART

As you begin, take a moment to listen to the song "Lead Kindly Light" by Audrey Assad.

There is a lot of instruction and advice on the importance of examining your physical posture to protect you from pain or injury, but have you pondered and examined your "heart posture"? What might it look like for kindness to be your "heart posture"?

Sometimes, kindness can look real but may in fact be false kindness fuelled by pride from an impure "heart posture".

| *False Kindness:* | self-love; fuelled by pride – example of Judas Iscariot |
| *True Kindness:* | generous; freely given and impartial – example of Jesus |

Can you identify times when your "heart posture" of kindness is more like a heart of Judas than Jesus?

Explore the following passages and notice the things that flow out of a "heart posture" of kindness:

And do not bring sorrow to God's Holy Spirit by the way you live. Remember, he has identified you as his own, guaranteeing that you will be saved on the day of redemption. Get rid of all bitterness, rage, anger, harsh words, and slander, as well as all types of evil behavior. Instead, be kind to each other, tenderhearted, forgiving one another, just as God through Christ has forgiven you.

Ephesians 4:30-32

I tell you, love your enemies. Help and give without expecting a return. You'll never - I promise - regret it. Live out this God-created identity the way our Father lives toward us, generously and graciously, even when we're at our worst. Our Father is kind; you be kind.

Luke 6:35-36 (MSG)

You might like to write a prayer in response to your meditation or draw something that represents whatever God has brought to your awareness.

KINDNESS

ON RETREAT: EXPLORING THE FRUIT OF THE SPIRIT

PART 3: BEING USEFUL

As you begin, take a moment to listen to the song "Less Like Me" by Zach Williams.

Therefore, as God's chosen people, holy and dearly loved, clothe yourselves with compassion, kindness, humility, gentleness and patience.

Colossians 3:12 (NIV)

The Greek word used for kindness is *chrestos* which is most accurately translated as "useful". This is a lovely broader picture of what the gift of kindness can be and is also an unexpected description of what kindness usually is. This usefulness is demonstrated within the context of relationships. What can you do today or tomorrow as a rhythm of "usefulness" in your relationships?

We are going to apply the principles of the Prayer of Examen (described on page 163), but instead of looking at a day, we will seek God's insight and awareness into our relationships and how we might develop a rhythm of usefulness (kindness) in these relationships.

To begin, thank God for all the relationships in your life.

Spend some time noticing all those you have a regular relationship with - parents, nuclear family, extended family, church family, work, community, friends, enemies.

Ask God to help you notice those relationships where it is easy to be kind and those where it feels like hard work.

Ask God to help you notice the relationships he wants you to spend time prayerfully reflecting on.

Ask God to bring ideas to your mind of how you can develop a "rhythm of usefulness" for each of these people.

Thank God for His kindness to you and the gift of His Spirit to help you reflect this kindness to others.

Keep reminding me

*I know I'm not the centre of the world
and yet I live that way.
You keep waking me, shaking me
with all the persistence of love.
Keep reminding me when I forget
and set boundaries to my loving.
Have me look beyond my little patch
to the world of being truly neighbour.*

— Noel Davis, Love Finds a Way (2000) [19]

ON RETREAT: EXPLORING THE FRUIT OF THE SPIRIT

KINDNESS

GOODNESS

"God's goodness is the root of all goodness; and our goodness, if we have any, springs out of His goodness."

— *William Tyndale (c. 1494 – 1536)*

The Greek word for goodness is *agathōsynē* which means "an uprightness of heart and life". It's something that begins in our hearts and spreads into our lives.

When we think of goodness in this way, it's easy to imagine a spring, bubbling up from the ground and flowing out into a stream. Just like an underground spring, goodness starts somewhere deep within as a posture of the heart and its outpouring becomes evident in all aspects of our lives and relationships.

Goodness is not just about obeying the rules or being well behaved. Goodness is a response of the heart, motivated by an obedience to God's commandments that embodies a desire to help other people in this journey we all call life.

PART 1: GOD'S GOODNESS

As you begin, take a moment to listen to the song "Good Good Father" by Housefires.

Scripture tells us that God is good. It doesn't just say that God does good things, or that God can work things for good. It takes a step beyond circumstances and situations and declares that goodness is at the very core of who God is.

Give thanks to the Lord, for he is good!
His faithful love endures forever.

Psalm 107:1

The Lord is good to everyone.
He showers compassion on all his creation.

Psalm 145:9

For the Lord is good.
His unfailing love continues forever,
and his faithfulness continues to each generation.

Psalm 100:5

Taste and see that the Lord is good.
Oh, the joys of those who take refuge in him!

Psalm 34:8

We also see God's goodness demonstrated in His infinitely generous attitude towards us. Our salvation is testimony to the goodness that is central to His character.

Let's explore goodness, as an aspect of God's character using the practice of Lectio Divina (described on page 161) and the following passage:

> *Therefore, since we have been made right in God's sight by faith, we have peace with God because of what Jesus Christ our Lord has done for us. Because of our faith, Christ has brought us into this place of undeserved privilege where we now stand, and we confidently and joyfully look forward to sharing God's glory.*
>
> *We can rejoice, too, when we run into problems and trials, for we know that they help us develop endurance. And endurance develops strength of character, and character strengthens our confident hope of salvation. And this hope will not lead to disappointment. For we know how dearly God loves us, because he has given us the Holy Spirit to fill our hearts with his love.*
>
> *When we were utterly helpless, Christ came at just the right time and died for us sinners. Now, most people would not be willing to die for an upright person, though someone might perhaps be willing to die for a person who is especially good. But God showed his great love for us by sending Christ to die for us while we were still sinners. And since we have been made right in God's sight by the blood of Christ, he will certainly save us from God's condemnation. For since our friendship with God was restored by the death of his Son while we were still his enemies, we will certainly be saved through the life of his Son. So now we can rejoice in our wonderful new relationship with God because our Lord Jesus Christ has made us friends of God.*
>
> *Romans 8:1-11*

How do you experience God's goodness in these verses? What do you notice of God as you reflect? Are there new things? Or familiar things that come to mind?

GOODNESS

Does seeing your salvation as a demonstration of God's goodness bring a new awareness?

As you mediate on God's word, let the things that you notice move beyond your thoughts. Let them drop into your heart and as they do, pay attention to the feelings and bodily sensations that emerge.

ON RETREAT: EXPLORING THE FRUIT OF THE SPIRIT

GOODNESS

PART 2: GOOD TO ME

As you begin, take a moment to listen to the song "Good to Me" by Audrey Assad.

The inevitability of life is that things will go wrong, that disappointments, relationship issues, natural disasters and illness will happen in our own lives and in the lives of those around us.

Sometimes things just don't feel "good". And sometimes it can be hard to trust God's goodness when we, or the people we love are hurting.

Psalm 46 reminds us that amidst the storm, God comes closer to us than the storm ever could be. In life's hardest moments He doesn't let us go.

God is our refuge and strength,

always ready to help in times of trouble.

So we will not fear when earthquakes come

and the mountains crumble into the sea.

Let the oceans roar and foam.

Let the mountains tremble as the waters surge! Interlude

A river brings joy to the city of our God,

the sacred home of the Most High.

God dwells in that city; it cannot be destroyed.

From the very break of day, God will protect it.

The nations are in chaos,

and their kingdoms crumble!

God's voice thunders,
and the earth melts!
The Lord of Heaven's Armies is here among us;
the God of Israel is our fortress. Interlude
Come, see the glorious works of the Lord:
See how he brings destruction upon the world.
He causes wars to end throughout the earth.
He breaks the bow and snaps the spear;
he burns the shields with fire.
"Be still, and know that I am God!
I will be honored by every nation.
I will be honored throughout the world."
The Lord of Heaven's Armies is here among us;
the God of Israel is our fortress.

Psalm 46

Take a moment to recall a time when something didn't work out how you had hoped or expected. It may have been a period of illness, a work disappointment, a relationship issue. It could be something that impacted you or someone you love.
- Close your eyes and sit quietly for a few minutes. Ask God to remind you of this time.
- How did you feel in yourself? What was your response to the situation? What was your response to God?
- How did you move through this situation? What were your feelings as you navigated it? Did you feel close to God during this time? Or did He feel distant?

Now, take a moment to recall a time when something went well. It may have been an event, a success that you celebrated or a joyful period of your life. It could be something that you personally experienced or something that occurred in the life of someone close to you.
- Again, close your eyes and sit quietly for a few minutes. Ask God to remind you of this time.
- How did you feel in yourself? What was your response to the situation? What was your response to God?
- How did you move through this situation? What were your feelings as you navigated it? Did you feel close to God during this time? Or did He feel distant?

What might God what you to notice as you reflect on these periods of difficulty and joy? Maybe it's something about you? Or about others? What does it reveal to you about God?

How might you hold both experiences together with the truth of God's goodness?

From the tears of my confession
That flowed with the touch of His kiss
It was this
His caress, His compassion
That compelled me
To journey deep inside
Where all the beauty of forgiveness hides
Asleep and silent, still
Until aroused and summoned at His will.

At times it seemed I journeyed all alone.
'Twas I that lost my way.
For faith and trust eluded me
And fear engulfed me
In a darkness so profound
That all my senses rose then fell
And mocked me with their falsehoods.
Then died to temporal things
In silence, without a sound.

Yet, in the darkest midnight,
My only light, that of my heart's desire,
My every substance melted by its fire,
I recognised the Stranger, my Beloved,
My Companion through the years.
For sense and intellect were gone.
In His eternity of forgiveness,
My faith grew strong, my fears grew dim
And there was nothing, nothing, nothing
Only Him.

— Betty W. Skinner, The Hidden Life (2006) [20]

GOODNESS

PART 3: THE GOOD SAMARITAN

Christ has no body now but yours,
No hands, no feet on earth but yours,
Yours are the eyes with which he looks
With compassion on this world.

Yours are the feet with which he walks to do good,
Yours are the hands, with which he blesses all the world,
Yours are the hands, yours are the feet.
Yours are the eyes, you are his body.

Christ has no body now but yours,
No hands, no feet on earth but yours,
Yours are the eyes with which he looks
With compassion on this world.
Christ has no body now on earth but yours.

— *Teresa of Avila (1515–1582)*

agathōsynē (a-gath-o-soon) = "an uprightness of heart and life"

Goodness begins as a posture of the heart – as an attitude of devotion to God and a deep desire for obedience to Him. From this starting point, goodness naturally flows into all aspects of our lives and relationships.

An example of someone who embodied goodness as "an uprightness of heart and life" is the Good Samaritan. Let's reflect on the following passage of scripture by engaging our imaginations (as described on page 165).

On one occasion an expert in the law stood up to test Jesus. "Teacher," he asked, "what must I do to inherit eternal life?"

"What is written in the Law?" he replied. "How do you read it?"

He answered, "'Love the Lord your God with all your heart and with all your soul and with all your strength and with all your mind'; and, 'Love your neighbor as yourself.'"

"You have answered correctly," Jesus replied. "Do this and you will live."

But he wanted to justify himself, so he asked Jesus, "And who is my neighbor?"

In reply Jesus said: "A man was going down from Jerusalem to Jericho, when he was attacked by robbers. They stripped him of his clothes, beat him and went away, leaving him half dead. A priest happened to be going down the same road, and when he saw the man, he passed by on the other side. So too, a Levite, when he came to the place and saw him, passed by on the other side. But a Samaritan, as he traveled, came where the man was; and when he saw him, he took pity on him. He went to him and bandaged his wounds, pouring on oil and wine. Then he put the man on his own donkey, brought him to an inn and took care of him. The next day he took out two denarii and gave them to the innkeeper. 'Look after him,' he said, 'and when I return, I will reimburse you for any extra expense you may have.'

"Which of these three do you think was a neighbor to the man who fell into the hands of robbers?"

The expert in the law replied, "The one who had mercy on him."

Jesus told him, "Go and do likewise."

Luke 10:25-37 (NIV)

ON RETREAT: EXPLORING THE FRUIT OF THE SPIRIT

GOODNESS

FAITHFULNESS

The Weave of Miracles

Praise be to you, gracious God,
  for this day, this earth, this life,
    for the weave of miracles blessing us
      and for your quiet power sustaining us.

We praise you for times of laughter and tears,
  risk and reconciliation,
    reflection and healing,
  and for the stubborn presence of your Spirit
    making it all sacred.

Praise be to you, awesome God,
  for the holy mysteries
    of our struggling and wondering,
  for our trials and triumphs,
    and all that moves us to awe,
      to love, to pray, to serve,
  since it is your Spirit that moves us so
    and is creating us still;
      through our Lord Jesus Christ. Amen.

  — *Ted Loder, My Heart in my Mouth (2013)* [21]

FAITHFULNESS

The very core of faithfulness in our faith, is believing that God is Who He says He is and continuing in that belief. We trust God will work out everything for good. We trust He will work His will in us, and we trust that no matter what happens on earth there is a future reward waiting for us in heaven. The only way we can have such faith is by the Holy Spirit's work in us as He testifies to the truth and urges us to seek God.

In Galatians 5, faithfulness sits in the list of the fruit that flow from God's Spirit working in and gifting us. Faithfulness is a key attribute of God's very nature. God is faithful! There is a concept of an enduring, never-ending element of relationship in faithfulness, but it is more than just this as it also describes who that person is, in the enduring. It is like an "entwining" together of lives in a journey of faithfulness both with God and with those around us. Faithfulness holds a deep sense of safety in this entwining covenant.

Faithfulness is a broad concept, and we are going to explore it through three aspects of relationships: keeping your promises, being steady in affection and remaining constant.

We are going to explore each of these aspects through God's example and then reflect on them in our own lives. For each part of this fruit, there will be a rhythm of following a Lectio Divina (described on page 161) through a passage showing us the expression in God, and then an Examen (described on page 163) as we reflect personally.

PART 1: KEEPING YOUR PROMISES

As you begin, take a moment to listen to the song "Promises" by Maverick City Music.

Lectio Divina

One of the very hallmark stories of God keeping His promises, is His promise to Abraham (initially Abram before God changed his name). Abraham's story picks up with his family settling in Haran and it is here, after the death of his father, God's call and promise to Abraham is first recorded. Then the journey of God's faithfulness starts to slowly but surely unfold. Abraham ended up having two sons, his son Isaac fathered Jacob, and Jacob fathered twelve sons of his own. These sons grew to become the twelve tribes of Israel - a great and mighty nation. God kept His promise to Abraham and through Abraham also to us.

Let's explore the following passages using the method of Lectio Divina (described on page 161):

The Lord had said to Abram, "Leave your native country, your relatives, and your father's family, and go to the land that I will show you. I will make you into a great nation. I will bless you and make you famous, and you will be a blessing to others. I will bless those who bless you and curse those who treat you with contempt. All the families on earth will be blessed through you."

So Abram departed as the Lord had instructed, and Lot went with him. Abram was seventy-five years old when he left Haran. He took his wife, Sarai, his nephew Lot, and all his wealth—his livestock and all the people he had taken into his household at Haran—and headed for the land of Canaan. When they arrived in Canaan, Abram traveled through the land as far as Shechem. There he set up camp beside the oak of Moreh. At that time, the area was inhabited by Canaanites.

Then the Lord appeared to Abram and said, "I will give this land to your descendants." And Abram built an altar there and dedicated it to the Lord, who had appeared to him. After that, Abram traveled south and set up camp in the hill country, with Bethel to the west and Ai to the east. There he built another altar and dedicated it to the Lord, and he worshiped the Lord. Then Abram continued traveling south by stages toward the Negev.

Genesis 12:1-9

This is the written account of the descendants of Adam. When God created human beings, he made them to be like himself. He created them male and female, and he blessed them and called them "human."

When Adam was 130 years old, he became the father of a son who was just like him—in his very image. He named his son Seth. After the birth of Seth, Adam lived another 800 years, and he had other sons and daughters. Adam lived 930 years, and then he died.

When Seth was 105 years old, he became the father of Enosh. After the birth of Enosh, Seth lived another 807 years, and he had other sons and daughters.

Genesis 5:1-7

The Lord kept his word and did for Sarah exactly what he had promised. She became pregnant, and she gave birth to a son for Abraham in his old age. This happened at just the time God had said it would. And Abraham named their son Isaac. Eight days after Isaac was born, Abraham circumcised him as God had commanded. Abraham was 100 years old when Isaac was born.

And Sarah declared, "God has brought me laughter. All who hear about this will laugh with me. Who would have said to Abraham that Sarah would nurse a baby? Yet I have given Abraham a son in his old age!"

Genesis 21:1-7

What catches your attention as you read God's unfolding promise in this story?

It was 25 years before Abraham fathered Isaac - a long wait. How do you feel as you consider this?

In this original promise to Abraham, God is also announcing His promise of the Gospel - not just to His chosen people, the Israelites, but also to the Gentiles, to each of us.

Scripture foresaw that God would justify the Gentiles by faith and announced the gospel in advance to Abraham: "All nations will be blessed through you".

Galatians 3:8

How does the "enduring" of God's promise of the Gospel touch your heart afresh today?

Take a moment to rest quietly in God's faithfulness.

Prayer of Examen

Let's now reflect on how this aspect of faithfulness is expressed in our own lives. We will use the framework of the Prayer of Examen (described on page 163) along with the suggestions that follow.

Thank your faithful God for all the "promise-keeping" memories you have of your journey of faith with Him.

FAITHFULNESS

Ask the Holy Spirit to lead you through a process of recalling the promises you have made to others in recent times and maybe also in longer memories.

As you notice these promises, allow yourself to also notice how you have maintained a commitment to these promises. Have you kept your promises? How has that impacted those relationships? Has that been hard work sometimes / often? How do you feel about your part in these promises? Do you find yourself making promises too readily before counting the cost? If you haven't kept promises what has contributed to this? Do you see your fruit of faithfulness as a "promise-keeper"? Do you notice a pattern in your "promise-keeping"?

Repent of any of those times when you have not demonstrated faithfulness and know the gift of God's forgiveness and the fresh empowering of His Spirit.

What specific things do you need to address that will help faithfulness, a fruit of God's Spirit bloom in your relationships with others?

ON RETREAT: EXPLORING THE FRUIT OF THE SPIRIT

FAITHFULNESS

PART 2: BEING STEADY IN AFFECTION

As you begin, take a moment to listen to the song "Reckless Love" by Cory Ashbury.

Lectio Divina

Jesus life on earth is a living picture of God's steady affection for His people, as He took on flesh and blood to show us God, and in His interactions with individuals sharing His humanity. At the very end of His life, we see Jesus "steady in affection", for those very close friends and disciples He had taught and journeyed with, through their intimate celebration of the Passover on the eve of Jesus' betrayal and crucifixion.

Let's explore the following passage using the method of Lectio Divina (described on page 161):

Before the Passover celebration, Jesus knew that his hour had come to leave this world and return to his Father. He had loved his disciples during his ministry on earth, and now he loved them to the very end. It was time for supper, and the devil had already prompted Judas, son of Simon Iscariot, to betray Jesus. Jesus knew that the Father had given him authority over everything and that he had come from God and would return to God. So he got up from the table, took off his robe, wrapped a towel around his waist, and poured water into a basin. Then he began to wash the disciples' feet, drying them with the towel he had around him.

When Jesus came to Simon Peter, Peter said to him, "Lord, are you going to wash my feet?"

Jesus replied, "You don't understand now what I am doing, but someday you will."

"No," Peter protested, "you will never ever wash my feet!"

Jesus replied, "Unless I wash you, you won't belong to me."

Simon Peter exclaimed, "Then wash my hands and head as well, Lord, not just my feet!"

Jesus replied, "A person who has bathed all over does not need to wash, except for the feet, to be entirely clean. And you disciples are clean, but not all of you." For Jesus knew who would betray him. That is what he meant when he said, "Not all of you are clean."

After washing their feet, he put on his robe again and sat down and asked, "Do you understand what I was doing? You call me 'Teacher' and 'Lord,' and you are right, because that's what I am. And since I, your Lord and Teacher, have washed your feet, you ought to wash each other's feet. I have given you an example to follow. Do as I have done to you. I tell you the truth, slaves are not greater than their master. Nor is the messenger more important than the one who sends the message. Now that you know these things, God will bless you for doing them.

"I am not saying these things to all of you; I know the ones I have chosen. But this fulfills the Scripture that says, 'The one who eats my food has turned against me.' I tell you this beforehand, so that when it happens you will believe that I am the Messiah. I tell you the truth, anyone who welcomes my messenger is welcoming me, and anyone who welcomes me is welcoming the Father who sent me."

Now Jesus was deeply troubled, and he exclaimed, "I tell you the truth, one of you will betray me!"

The disciples looked at each other, wondering whom he could mean. The disciple Jesus loved was sitting next to Jesus at the table. Simon Peter motioned to him to ask, "Who's he talking about?" So that disciple leaned over to Jesus and asked, "Lord, who is it?"

Jesus responded, "It is the one to whom I give the bread I dip in the bowl." And when he had dipped it, he gave it to Judas, son of Simon Iscariot. When Judas had eaten the bread, Satan entered into him. Then Jesus told him, "Hurry and do what you're going to do." None of the others at the table knew what Jesus meant. Since Judas was their treasurer, some thought Jesus was telling him to go and pay for the food or to give some money to the poor. So Judas left at once, going out into the night.

As soon as Judas left the room, Jesus said, "The time has come for the Son of Man to enter into his glory, and God will be glorified because of him. And since God receives glory because of the Son, he will give his own glory to the Son, and he will do so at once. Dear children, I will be with you only a little longer. And as I told the Jewish leaders, you will search for me, but you can't come where I am going. So now I am giving you a new commandment: Love each other. Just as I have loved you, you should love each other. Your love for one another will prove to the world that you are my disciples."

John 13:1-35

What catches your attention as you read God's steadiness in affection seen in Jesus' love for His disciples?

Verse 1 declares, "He loved them to the end". How does this phrase impact you?

Can you imagine yourself at this celebration meal with Jesus, and Him reaching down to wash your feet? How do you respond to this gesture?

Loving them to the end also included Judas, the betrayer. What example of "being steady in affection" does this example unfold for you?

Take a moment to rest quietly in God's faithfulness.

Prayer of Examen

Let's now reflect on how this aspect of faithfulness is expressed in our own lives. We will use the framework of the Prayer of Examen (described on page 163) along with the suggestions that follow.

Thank your faithful God for His "steadiness in affection" for you.

Ask the Holy Spirit to lead you through a process of recalling relationships around you and notice your "steadiness of affection" for these people in your life.

In which relationships do you find it harder to maintain a "steadiness of affection"? What things impact your "steadiness of affection" with others? Who has clearly demonstrated to you an example of "steadiness in affection"?

Repent of any of those times when you have not demonstrated faithfulness and know the gift of God's forgiveness and the fresh empowering of His Spirit.

What specific things do you need to address that will help faithfulness, a fruit of God's Spirit bloom in your relationships with others?

FAITHFULNESS

PART 3: REMAINING CONSTANT

As you begin, take a moment to listen to the song "Firm Foundation" by Cody Carnes.

Lectio Divina

Through the Psalms we read a myriad of descriptions about God's constant presence with His people - our confidence, stronghold, hope, strong tower, refuge, joy and protection. Today we are going to focus on Psalm 91. Let's explore this passage using the method of Lectio Divina (described on page 161):

Those who live in the shelter of the Most High

will find rest in the shadow of the Almighty.

This I declare about the Lord:

He alone is my refuge, my place of safety;

he is my God, and I trust him.

For he will rescue you from every trap

and protect you from deadly disease.

He will cover you with his feathers.

He will shelter you with his wings.

His faithful promises are your armor and protection.

Do not be afraid of the terrors of the night,

nor the arrow that flies in the day.

Do not dread the disease that stalks in darkness,

nor the disaster that strikes at midday.

Though a thousand fall at your side,

though ten thousand are dying around you,
these evils will not touch you.
Just open your eyes,
and see how the wicked are punished.
If you make the Lord your refuge,
if you make the Most High your shelter,
no evil will conquer you;
no plague will come near your home.
For he will order his angels
to protect you wherever you go.
They will hold you up with their hands
so you won't even hurt your foot on a stone.
You will trample upon lions and cobras;
you will crush fierce lions and serpents under your feet!
The Lord says, "I will rescue those who love me.
I will protect those who trust in my name.
When they call on me, I will answer;
I will be with them in trouble.
I will rescue and honor them.
I will reward them with a long life
and give them my salvation."

Psalm 91

What catches your attention as you read of God's constant presence?

Which description of God in this passage holds the strongest meaning for you? Why do you think this might be?

In verse 14 it says, "I will set you in a high place, safe and secure before my face". How does this picture of constant safety in God's presence speak to your heart, even in the hard times?

Take a moment to rest quietly in God's faithfulness.

Prayer of Examen

Let's now reflect on how this aspect of faithfulness is expressed in our own lives. We will use the framework of the Prayer of Examen (described on page 163) along with the suggestions that follow.

Thank your faithful God for "remaining constant" with you.

Ask the Holy Spirit to lead you through a process of noticing those difficult times when you have needed people to "remain constant" for you and when you have decided to "remain constant" for others.

How have these experiences of faithfulness impacted you? Do you find it easy to "remain constant" for others? Or do you find yourself becoming bored, faint-hearted, disillusioned, distracted? How does God's Spirit want to speak to you in this? Is there someone in your life right now that God is inviting you to "remain constant" with?

Repent of any of those times when you have not demonstrated faithfulness and know the gift of God's forgiveness and the fresh empowering of His Spirit.

What specific things do you need to address that will help faithfulness bloom in your relationships with others?

FAITHFULNESS

ON RETREAT: EXPLORING THE FRUIT OF THE SPIRIT

GENTLENESS

> *"Once in a while we meet a gentle person. Gentleness is a virtue hard to find in a society that admires toughness and roughness. [...] Gentle is the one who does 'not break the crushed reed, or snuff the faltering wick.' Gentle is the one who is attentive to the strengths and weaknesses of the other and enjoys being together more than accomplishing something. A gentle person treads lightly, listens carefully, looks tenderly, and touches with reverence. A gentle person knows that true growth requires nurture, not force. Let's dress ourselves with gentleness."*
>
> — Henri Nouwen, *Bread for the Journey* (2007) [22]

Of all the fruit of the Spirit, gentleness can be particularly challenging to understand and to practice. Often associated with weakness or passivity, gentleness is overlooked in our culture that favours assertiveness and the needs of an individual. Yet, the Bible frames gentleness as a quality that is both powerful and important in our relationship with God and with others.

If we think about gentleness in terms of its opposites, we find that it is countered by a desire for revenge, a sense of self-importance, or the expression of anger. Gentleness requires humility – a deep recognition that others are loved by God as much as we are. Gentleness necessitates reverent compassion – a genuine love and respect for what God has created. Gentleness involves nurturing – the expression of tenderness, empathy, forgiveness, kindness and patience. Gentleness is a strength, not a weakness.

PART 1: HUMILITY

As you begin, take a moment to listen to the song "Humble" by Audrey Assad.

Gentleness comes from a state of humility. People who lack gentleness can often be prideful, easily angered, or feel the need for revenge.

Someone who is gentle wants to help others, even when they have been wronged. Gentleness allows us to see the worth that God places in others and recognise that they are loved by God just as much as we are.

An example of gentleness can be seen in John 8, when the Pharisees bring a woman who was caught in adultery to Jesus. The Pharisees tell Jesus that the Law of Moses commands them to stone such a woman, to which Jesus responds, "Let any one of you who is without sin be the first to throw a stone at her" (John 8:7).

After everyone leaves, Jesus does not condemn the woman. He simply says to her, "Go now and leave your life of sin" (John 8:11).

Just as Jesus was gentle with the woman in this story, God is gentle with us. Even in our sin, He continues to love us. He does not keep a record of our wrongs but offers forgiveness if we come to Him.

Let's reflect on this passage of scripture in John by engaging our imaginations (described on page 165).

Jesus returned to the Mount of Olives, but early the next morning he was back again at the Temple. A crowd soon gathered, and he sat down and taught them. As he was speaking, the teachers of religious law and the Pharisees brought a woman who had been caught in the act of adultery. They put her in front of the crowd.

"Teacher," they said to Jesus, "this woman was caught in the act of adultery. The law of Moses says to stone her. What do you say?"

They were trying to trap him into saying something they could use against him, but Jesus stooped down and wrote in the dust with his finger. They kept demanding an answer, so he stood up again and said, "All right, but let the one who has never sinned throw the first stone!" Then he stooped down again and wrote in the dust.

When the accusers heard this, they slipped away one by one, beginning with the oldest, until only Jesus was left in the middle of the crowd with the woman. Then Jesus stood up again and said to the woman, "Where are your accusers? Didn't even one of them condemn you?"

"No, Lord," she said.

And Jesus said, "Neither do I. Go and sin no more."

John 8:1-11

Speak to my heart, Lord,
that it might be Yours
though it be unworthy,
ant-like in its capacity,
infinitesimal in its glory.
Bless that part of it that is You.
Let it light the darkness of this,
a barren world.

— *Betty W. Skinner, The Circle of Love (2006)* [23]

GENTLENESS

ON RETREAT: EXPLORING THE FRUIT OF THE SPIRIT

PART 2: REVERENT COMPASSION

As you begin, take a moment to listen to the song "A Thousand Hallelujahs" by Brooke Ligertwood.

The Addis Ababa Fistula hospital, set up by Reg and Catherine Hamlin in 1975, has cured tens of thousands of women who have suffered from childbirth related injuries in Ethiopia. Central to patient care was the reverent compassion that these surgeons expressed in treating their patients - their genuine love for each person who came to them for help and the deep respect that they showed each patient as they recognised them as a child of God.

The Hamlins embodied gentleness as they cared for, nurtured and loved their patients. They showed the injured women who came through the hospital doors that they had worth in a society that treated them as outcasts and the gentle spirit with which they ministered gave their patients hope.

Take a moment to recall a time when you have seen "reverent compassion" in action – perhaps it was shown to you, maybe it was a situation you witnessed, or a time that you showed reverent compassion to another person.
- Close your eyes and sit quietly for a few minutes. Ask God to remind you of this time.
- How did you feel as this situation unfolded?
- How do you feel now as you recall this situation? Are there any fresh things God might want to show you?

Take a moment to recall a time when you didn't show "reverent compassion" to another person.
- Close your eyes and sit quietly for a few minutes. Ask God to remind you of this time.
- How did you feel as this situation unfolded?

- How do you feel now as you recall this situation? Are there any fresh things God might want to show you?

Is reverent compassion - genuine love and respect for God's people - something that flows easily in your relationships and interactions with others?

*Lakes are mirrors, God's mirrors in His earth
consistently reflecting such beautiful things.
The trees, the clouds, the morning sun, the moon,
God's creation and all the lakes' reflections
seem to lead upward.*

*Eyes are mirrors, too,
God's mirrors in His people.
What do yours reflect?
Are they soft and warm and gentle,
leading others upward, reflecting Christ,
The Perfect Image, the reason for our mirrors?*

— Betty W. Skinner, The Circle of Love (2006) [24]

ON RETREAT: EXPLORING THE FRUIT OF THE SPIRIT

GENTLENESS

PART 3: NURTURING

Gentleness also involves nurturing. It is an outward expression of tenderness, empathy, forgiveness, kindness and patience that builds and grows and strengthens others. Gentleness is life-giving. It fortifies others, nourishes them and has the power to effect change. Gentleness is like a shawl, that when worn, flows softly and wraps everyone it touches in safety and tenderness.

The following passages of Scripture give us a picture of Jesus' gentle and nurturing way. Take some time to reflect on these verses. You may like to use the practice of Lectio Divina (described on page 161) as you ask God to show you what He might like you to notice as you take this time with Him.

Aware of this, Jesus withdrew from that place. A large crowd followed him, and he healed all who were ill. He warned them not to tell others about him. This was to fulfill what was spoken through the prophet Isaiah:

"Here is my servant whom I have chosen,

the one I love, in whom I delight;

I will put my Spirit on him,

and he will proclaim justice to the nations.

He will not quarrel or cry out;

no one will hear his voice in the streets.

A bruised reed he will not break,

and a smoldering wick he will not snuff out,

till he has brought justice through to victory.

In his name the nations will put their hope."

Matthew 12:15-21

"Come to me, all you who are weary and burdened, and I will give you rest. Take my yoke upon you and learn from me, for I am gentle and humble in heart, and you will find rest for your souls. For my yoke is easy and my burden is light."

Matthew 11:28-30

He tends his flock like a shepherd:
  He gathers the lambs in his arms
and carries them close to his heart;
  he gently leads those that have young.

Isaiah 40:11

Can you picture yourself wearing a shawl of gentleness? Imagine yourself putting on the shawl. What does it look like? What does it feel like? How does wearing this shawl shape the way you interact with others?

GENTLENESS

SELF-CONTROL

But the Holy Spirit produces this kind of fruit in our lives: love, joy, peace, patience, kindness, goodness, faithfulness, gentleness, and self-control. There is no law against these things!

Galatians 5:22-23

Self-control is the last in the list of the fruit of the Spirit in Galatians 5:22-23. Many of the other fruit seem like a process of opening up and out-pouring. But this fruit feels like a "reigning in". Maybe it appears as the crown of the list of fruit, because exercising self-control – having a controlled self – helps the out-pouring of all the other fruit. Controlling our ego, passion, desires (our "flesh") so that all the other fruit can flow out from a heart walking in step with God's Spirit!

PART 1: WHY DO WE NEED SELF-CONTROL?

As you begin, take a moment to listen to the song "Canticle" by TAYA.

Have you heard of the "marshmallow test"? Walter Mischel conducted an experiment to see how children responded to being left alone with a marshmallow for fifteen minutes, instructing them that if they didn't eat the marshmallow, they would be given two. This famous experiment from nearly fifty years ago demonstrated that those young children who waited the longest went on to have higher scores at the end of school than those who couldn't wait. But not only this, in their later years they were thinner, earned more advanced degrees, used fewer drugs, and coped better with stress! Their ability to exercise self-control with a marshmallow as a child was an indicator of their ability to make better choices for their life as adults.

Proverbs 25:28 compares someone without self-control to a "city broken into and left without walls". In the Bible, self-control is not about rules and restrictions but about mastering our desires rather than being mastered by them.

Struggling with self-control shows us what the Bible describes as the "flesh". Whatever has control over us is our master. Timothy Keller describes the "flesh" as the "bent" of your whole person to be the centre of the universe. In contrast, God's Spirit, is like a flame torch gradually softening the "bent rod" of your life and bending you back upright in line with God's desires – like a kind of "cosmic orthodontics".[25]

Read the following verses which highlight the harm of being controlled by the "flesh":

You say, "I am allowed to do anything"—but not everything is good for you. And even though "I am allowed to do anything," I must not become a slave to anything.

I Corinthians 6:12

The sinful nature wants to do evil, which is just the opposite of what the Spirit wants. And the Spirit gives us desires that are the opposite of what the sinful nature desires. These two forces are constantly fighting each other, so you are not free to carry out your good intentions.

Galatians 5:17

So letting your sinful nature control your mind leads to death. But letting the Spirit control your mind leads to life and peace.

Romans 8:6

What things stand out to you as you read through these verses?

The "flesh" is the sinful part of our nature; the part not controlled by God's Spirit. It could be understood as those things you are striving for to give you a certain amount of control over your life. The "flesh" makes us want to be our own god, rather than trusting God who is in control.

In Romans, Paul wants us to understand the difference of living under the condemning weight of the law compared to the freedom of living with Christ. In Chapter 8 he describes the power of the life-giving Spirit of God (who gifts us with self-control), compared to living under the law. Spend some time reading through these verses and allow God's Spirit to touch your heart with the truth.

So now there is no condemnation for those who belong to Christ Jesus. And because you belong to him, the power of the life-giving Spirit has freed you from the power of sin that leads to death. The law of Moses was unable to save us because of the weakness of our sinful nature. So God did what the law could not do. He sent his own Son in a body like the bodies we sinners have. And in that body God declared an end to sin's control over us by giving his Son as a sacrifice for our sins. He did this so that the just requirement of the law would be fully satisfied for us, who no longer follow our sinful nature but instead follow the Spirit.

Those who are dominated by the sinful nature think about sinful things, but those who are controlled by the Holy Spirit think about things that please the Spirit. So letting your sinful nature control your mind leads to death. But letting the Spirit control your mind leads to life and peace. For the sinful nature is always hostile to God. It never did obey God's laws, and it never will. That's why those who are still under the control of their sinful nature can never please God.

But you are not controlled by your sinful nature. You are controlled by the Spirit if you have the Spirit of God living in you. (And remember that those who do not have the Spirit of Christ living in them do not belong to him at all.) And Christ lives within you, so even though your body will die because of sin, the Spirit gives you life because you have been made right with God. The Spirit of God, who raised Jesus from the dead, lives in you. And just as God raised Christ Jesus from the dead, he will give life to your mortal bodies by this same Spirit living within you.

Therefore, dear brothers and sisters, you have no obligation to do what your sinful nature urges you to do. For if you live by its dictates, you will die. But if through the power of the Spirit you put to death the deeds of your sinful nature, you will live. For all who are led by the Spirit of God are children of God.

So you have not received a spirit that makes you fearful slaves. Instead, you received God's Spirit when he adopted you as his own children. Now we call him, "Abba, Father." For his Spirit joins with our spirit to affirm that we are God's children. And since we are his children, we are his heirs. In fact, together with Christ we are heirs of God's glory. But if we are to share his glory, we must also share his suffering.

Romans 8:1-17

What fresh insights about self-control do you notice as you read this passage?

Self-control as a spiritual gift, is produced in and through us by God's Spirit. This self-control isn't whipped up from within us by our own efforts and willpower. We are energised and empowered by God's Spirit. Controlling ourselves is about being "controlled by Christ" (2 Corinthians 5:14), not just bringing our "fleshly" desires under our own control, but under the control of Christ by the power of His Spirit. Self-control is surrender.

You might like to write out a prayer in response to these things you have reflected on.

*I see a message in the spider's web
and its reflection in the sun.
Watch it.
One second it glistens,
the next second it's gone.
Is not our walk through life
with Christ like this?
One second we are so very close,
all things glisten.
the next second we stumble,
stagger, fall, are lost.
Why?
Because in this second second
our selfish self blocks out the glisten.*

— Betty W. Skinner, The Circle of Love (2006) [26]

ON RETREAT: EXPLORING THE FRUIT OF THE SPIRIT

SELF-CONTROL

PART 2: WHERE DO YOU NEED TO EXERCISE MORE SELF-CONTROL?

As you begin, take a moment to listen to the song "So Help Me God" by Benjamin William Hastings.

Each of us is unique. We have our own unique fingerprints and our own unique desires and temptations. Everyone's "flesh" is a different shape. So, each of us will also have different (and maybe similar) areas of life where we need to practice exercising more self-control than others.

The Prayer of Examen (described on page 163) is a prayer tool that can be used to review our recent past and to seek an awareness of God in our daily life. It can be used as a reflective practice each day and it can also be used to review a pattern of something specific over a wider span of time in our lives - a process of reflecting on our day-to-day life, together with God's Spirit, in a slower, focused, considered way and being aware of Gods' grace guiding and holding us in the process.

We are going to use the Prayer of Examen with the focus of asking God to help us notice those areas in our life where we are struggling to exercise self-control and then asking Him to guide and empower us specifically in those spaces.

Begin by giving God thanks for all the things you are grateful for today.

Allow your mind to wander as you reflect on the ways God has blessed you this last week. What emerges as you reflect? Big things, small things, the gift of faith, work, food, friends and more.

Ask God to fill you afresh with His Spirit and to lead you through the soul searching of self-control awareness. Ask Him to hold you in this process so that you might not hide in denial, wallow in self-pity or seethe in self-loathing.

Try closing your eyes and look back at your life over the last few weeks. Look through each day like you are watching a movie of your life replaying before you. Start in the morning at the beginning of the week and work through the day to the evening and then repeat for the next day, asking God to point out those moments when you identify that you have needed to exercise more self-control.

At those moments, let it be like pressing "pause" on the movie, to sit with the moment for a thorough awareness of the situation, triggers, background and feelings. You might like to write the moment down.

Then press "play" and continue through until today.

Look through the list. Is there a pattern that you notice? In circumstances, time of the day, the person, or a particular day? Notice any patterns and pray for wisdom in this awareness.

Ask God to forgive you for those times self-control has been lacking.

Ask God for healing for any harm that maybe have been done.

Ask God for wisdom to discern how you might be better able to handle those moments, people, days or times in the future.

Think and pray through the upcoming week or fortnight ahead.

Ask God to help you to imagine the things you'll be doing, the people you'll see and the decisions you'll be mulling over. Ask God to help you exercise self-control with any moments that you foresee might be difficult.

And You Wait

I wanted to do my own thing.
And You let me.
After all,
You gave me this will.
This floundering will
that gives me
a sense of me
a sense of control
a sense of choice.

And You wait.

You wait like a father who gives
his girl a new bike
and she goes missing
for hours.

You wait like a father who gives
his son his inheritance
knowing he'll make a mess
of things.

And you wait.

You wait on the street till dusk,
sure that she'll come home
before the darkness sets in.

*You wait at the gate and run
when you see his sunken soul
stagger into the city.*

And You welcome.

*You welcome the strong-of-will.
The rebellious heart.
The limit-tester.
The boundary-pusher.
The bankrupt and broken.
You welcome any will
that comes home,
even for a short time.*

You welcome me.

*Your door is always open,
as are your arms.
The feast forever prepared.
Tears of joy ready to cross the threshold
of Your cheeks.*

*Father, Son and Spirit.
Creator of wills.
Your imitable will to love
and forgive
compels creation
to do the same.*

— David Tenson, The Wrestle (2020) [27]

SELF-CONTROL

ON RETREAT: EXPLORING THE FRUIT OF THE SPIRIT

PART 3: CHOOSING THE IMPORTANT OVER THE URGENT

As you begin, take a moment to listen to the song "Home" by Jeremy Riddle.

Timothy Keller suggests an explanation of self-control is "choosing the important thing over the urgent thing". [28] This is often difficult to identify and to carry through.

What are some of the things that feel "urgent" and vie for your attention regularly? How do we choose what is important?

Jesus explained that the greatest commandment is:

And you must love the Lord your God with all your heart, all your soul, all your mind, and all your strength.' The second is equally important: 'Love your neighbor as yourself.' No other commandment is greater than these."

Mark 12:30-31

IMPORTANT: Please God and give Him joy
URGENT: Please self and know joy apart from God

Paul describes this self-control "fruiting of the spirit", over the "unfruitfulness of the flesh", in the metaphor of running a race to gain a prize, in 1 Corinthians.

I do everything to spread the Good News and share in its blessings.

Don't you realize that in a race everyone runs, but only one person gets the prize? So run to win! All athletes are disciplined in their training. They do it to win a prize that will fade away, but we do it for an eternal prize. So I run with purpose in every step. I am not just shadowboxing. I discipline my body like an athlete, training it to do what it should. Otherwise, I fear that after preaching to others I myself might be disqualified.

1 Corinthians 9:23-27

What is that "prize"? The prize is eternal life:

I give them eternal life, and they shall never perish; no one will snatch them out of my hand. My Father, who has given them to me, is greater than all; no one can snatch them out of my Father's hand. I and the Father are one."

John 10:28-30

The prize is dwelling with God as His people:

I heard a loud shout from the throne, saying, "Look, God's home is now among his people! He will live with them, and they will be his people. God himself will be with them. He will wipe every tear from their eyes, and there will be no more death or sorrow or crying or pain. All these things are gone forever."

Revelation 21:3-4

The prize is a changed living experience:

They will never again be hungry or thirsty;
    they will never be scorched by the heat of the sun.
For the Lamb on the throne
    will be their Shepherd.
He will lead them to springs of life-giving water.
    And God will wipe every tear from their eyes."

Revelation 7:16-17

The prize is praise from Jesus for a life of obedience:

"The master was full of praise. 'Well done, my good and faithful servant. You have been faithful in handling this small amount, so now I will give you many more responsibilities. Let's celebrate together!'

Matthew 25:21

Spend some time reflecting on these truths and imagining them. Allow your mind to hold the truth and to transform it through your imagination, not just hearing the truth with your ears, but seeing it in your life.

Now, picture your life as a race. Picture yourself standing on the podium with the prize - a crown of eternal life. Picture the prize and the finish after all the hard work of training and preparation.

Your challenge now is to replay this vision in the moments of the urges of the "flesh". Replay this image of the "prize" when the Spirit's fruit of self-control is helping you identify the difference between the important and the urgent - at those times you are tempted to be distracted by your own joy and control, away from God's eternal prize.

Now return to some of those places you noticed through the Prayer of Examen in the previous section, where you need to exercise more self-control. Sit with those situations alongside your fresh picture of the "prize" and allow yourself to experience the refreshing gift of God's Spirit of self-control.

The self-control that flows from the fruit of the Spirit doesn't just become a choice to exercise your willpower over things you want to control. This self-control is an outflowing of God's Spirit, as you wrestle with the desires of the "flesh" so that God remains in control as you focus on the important prize.

Help Me To Follow

*From the depths of my being
my heart cries out:
Help me to follow, Lord,
help me to follow.*

*Midst the noise of the world
be my silence
that I might listen and hear.
Then help me to follow, Lord,
help me to follow.*

*Midst the pull of the world
be my center
that I might abide and be still.
Then help me to follow, Lord,
help me to follow.*

*Midst the materialism of the world
be my simplicity
that I might become pure and be pleasing.
Then help me to follow, Lord,
help me to follow.*

— *Betty W. Skinner, The Circle of Love (2006)* [29]

SELF-CONTROL

LECTIO DIVINA

Lectio Divina (Latin for "divine reading") is a prayerful and reflective way to read God's word. Rather than seeking an intellectual understanding of the text, the reader seeks instead to engage with the inspirer of the text: God. Reading with the heart is about giving God room to move at the deepest level. The process of Lectio Divina is outlined below.

Silencio - Preparation

It is helpful to begin with some moments of silence; move from the busyness of the day to time with God. This allows us to "change gears", to slow down, to prepare our hearts to receive God's word. Sit comfortably, close your eyes and relax with a few deep breaths. What is going through your mind? How are you feeling? Offer these thoughts and feelings to God. Ask Him to quieten your heart and enable you to become fully open to His Spirit today. Don't rush the quieting process. When you feel ready, begin.

Lectio – Reading

Read the passage slowly and attentively, gently listening for a word or phrase that seems to stand out or touch your heart. Ask God to show you what it is He has to say to you today through His Word. Read the passage through again, and again, gradually focusing on a particular phrase or verse which speaks to you especially. Read it as many times as you need.

Meditatio – Meditation

When you have found something that captures your attention or speaks to you in a personal way take it, ruminate on it, savour it. Allow it to penetrate deep within. As you mediate on God's word, let the things that you notice move beyond your thoughts. Let them drop into your heart and as they do, pay attention to the feelings and bodily sensations that emerge.

Oratio – Prayer

Respond to God spontaneously in prayer telling Him what you have been meditating on, offering Him your deepest thoughts and feelings without censoring them to what you think He wants to hear. If prayer doesn't flow naturally, then ask God to help you and if your thoughts stray ask Him to guide you back to the passage. If what He is revealing is not clear or is confusing, then ask for guidance. Thank Him for anything that touches your heart.

Contemplatio – Contemplation

Let go of your own words and allow yourself to sit quietly and attentively in God's presence. Listen, seeking to be open to anything God wants to say to you. In contemplation we stop our spiritual "doing" and simply "be". When ready, finish by thanking God.

The Prayer of Examen

The Prayer of Examen was gifted to us by St. Ignatius of Loyola, a 16th century theologian and mystic. This practice is an opportunity to prayerfully play back the events of the day, and instead of making our own analysis and judgements, we ask God to bring our awareness to whatever in the day He wants us to notice now – an event, person, mood or insight. As our awareness of these things unfolds, we seek God's invitation to our hearts.

Rest

Find a comfortable position. Take some time to relax, and become still, in body, mind and spirit. Take some slow, regular breaths and remind yourself of God's presence with you, through the Holy Spirit.

Reflect

Ask God to bring to your awareness the things that He wants you to notice. Gently play back your day. Just as you would press the pause button on a movie, linger on the people, places and happenings that catch your attention. Let them touch you again as you remember them. You may be surprised by what you notice - fear, anger, hurt, disgust, sadness, happiness, confidence, pride, contentment. As you re-experience your day and as people, places and events come to mind, ask God what He is saying to you through this awareness – be open to His leading.

Respond

Respond spontaneously and truthfully from your heart – with joy, gratitude, sadness, a cry for help, or perhaps a prayer of deepening trust – whatever is authentic for you.

IMAGINATIVE BIBLE READING

Our imaginations, used alongside the Gospels or any other passage of scripture, can draw us into a personal encounter with God as we connect with the story in this special way. The idea is to stop thinking of Biblical events from the outside and to visualise yourself on the inside, fully immersed in the story, just as you're fully a part of God's salvation story today.

Open in Prayer

Take a moment to pray. Ask God to guide you in your reflection and to help you notice where He might have something to say. Remember: The Holy Spirit lives within you and inspires you today.

Read the Passage

Read through the Bible passage. Read it a few times to get a sense of the setting and the development of the story.

Picture the Scene

Now allow the setting of the passage to appear before you as if you were there. Allow your mind to get an imaginative grasp of what would be sensed. You might like to use some of these questions as a framework for your exploration of the scene -
- What kind of "atmosphere" does the scene suggest? Inviting, threatening, vibrant? Does any part of the scene attract your

attention more?
- What seems to be happening in the scene?
- Who is there?
- What can you see, hear, smell, taste, feel as you imagine the scene?

Enter the Story

Now you are going to step into the story in your imagination. The story is now happening around you. Where do you find yourself? Without forcing anything, allow yourself to be drawn into the part of the story that is attracting you. Allow God to lead your imagining and trust that He will shine a light on what He wants you to notice.
- How are you feeling about what is happening in the scene? Disturbed? Attracted? Curious? Afraid? Eager?
- Do you identify with anyone in the story? Or do you feel like an outsider looking in? Who are you repelled by in the story? If it feels right, you may like to allow yourself to become one of the characters in the story.
- Do you feel drawn to speak to anyone there? What do you feel you want to say? What do you feel is being said to you?

Ending your Prayer

If you feel able to do so, end your prayer by entering a conversation with Jesus. Express your feelings about the experience, and let your heart be open to receive whatever God may want to suggest to you. When you are ready, close your prayer and spend a few minutes reflecting on the experience. You may want to write down your reflections or express them in some other way.

Suggestions for Group Leaders

Leading a small group can be both rewarding and challenging. As you facilitate your group, these are some things that may be helpful to consider:

Location

Select a place where you can easily accommodate everyone together in one space. You may like to set up chairs in a circle around a central focal point. This ensures that everyone can see you and feels equally a part of the group.

There should also be spaces where people can break away for time on their own. Places outside where group members may sit and reflect are ideal. For this reason, you may like to ask people to bring a folding chair, a hat and sunscreen with them.

Introduce the Topic and Group Members

When all members of the group have arrived, it is important to provide them with an opportunity to introduce themselves. Although they are on retreat with the intention of spending time on their own with God, they will do this in the company of others who share the journey with them. You may like to ask each person to say their name and offer a short explanation of what has brought them away on retreat.

During this initial time together, you can also introduce the topic for the day, explain the timetable, cover off other housekeeping items and set any expectations for the group.

Each session will follow the rhythm of coming together as a group for the introduction of that session. Individuals will then break away on their own to spend some time in silence with God. One important ground rule that we like to set is that this individual time should be alone. This allows each person the privilege of time in silence and solitude with God and minimises the likelihood of distraction for others.

The Program

Each part of the retreat is provided as a stimulus for reflection and a starting point for time with God. It should be held lightly. If participants are tired by the end of the day and simply need time to rest, then they should not feel guilty for doing so. If they begin one section of the program, but their heart calls them to continue exploring a previous part, then they should feel comfortable to do that. Similarly, if God lays something outside of the program on their hearts for their time alone with Him, then they should follow that prompt and set the program aside.

As the group gathers at the beginning of each part of the retreat, it can be helpful to share the key theme together along with any suggested music or to have someone read the poem or written prayer for that time. If you choose to listen to music as a group, then it can be helpful to bring a portable speaker or ensure that you have access to a sound system.

Each group member will need to have their own copy of this book to participate in the retreat.

Group Reflection

To conclude the day, it is helpful for the group to come together for a time of praise and thanksgiving. This is a space where group members can share something of the insights that God may have gifted them with during their time on retreat.

There should be no expectation for every group member to share during this time. Sharing is optional. It is an opportunity, not a necessity.

It should be made clear to the group that this is a confidential space and that anything shared is not to be spoken about outside the group. Participants should only share what they are comfortable with.

As you begin this time, start with some silence and invite group members to share when they are ready.

As each person shares, the group should listen without interruption and without reply. This is not a space for others to offer advice or to share their own similar stories. It is simply a platform for honouring what God has laid on each person's heart and to give Him praise for that new awareness.

Sometimes there can be tears as people share of their experience. Bring some tissues along just in case. Some people are more comfortable with tears (either as the one shedding them, or the one witnessing them) than others. The group should resist the temptation to rescue the person from their tears and simply hold and honour the tears as part of the story that has been shared.

After each person has shared, the group should hold them in silent prayer for a short time. The next person may begin when they are ready.

When it seems right, close the sharing time. You may like to pray for the group as they return home and back to their normal life. You may like to play a song to finish, or there may be something else that catches your heart as you conclude the day.

Suggestions For Individuals

As you take time away for retreat on your own, you may like to take the following things into consideration:

Time

The sample program outlined at the beginning of this book can be adjusted based on how much time you have available to spend on retreat. Obviously, the group introduction and reflection times can be omitted, and you may like to structure your day with less time for breaks. As an individual, you also have the freedom of being able to take more or less time with each session if that is what suits you.

Location

Find a place where you can be alone and won't be distracted by other people. If you enjoy taking time outside, then it may be suitable to spend the day at a park, by a lake, at the beach or somewhere else that provides you with a natural backdrop for contemplation. You might choose to spend your retreat time inside in a comfortable space.

If you choose to retreat at home, this can require some additional planning to ensure that elements of your normal life do not become impediments to your time alone with God. You may need to make a conscious decision to set aside any unfinished tasks for the day, to unplug the phone or to put away any other items that may serve as a distraction.

Share with a friend

After your time on retreat, it can be helpful to share any new insights or awareness with a friend. You might like to talk about your retreat time over coffee or while simply enjoying an activity together.

NOTES

1. Benner, J. (2011) Contemplative vision: A guide to Christian Art and Prayer. Downers Grove, IL: IVP Books.

2. From the article: Killigrew, A. (2013) 'Desert Spirituality', *Presence: An International Journal of Spiritual Direction*, Volume 19 No. 1: 62.

3. Skinner, B. W. (2006) The Hidden Life: Revelations of a Holy Journey. Colorado Springs, CO: Navpress.

4. Skinner, B. W. (2006) The Hidden Life: Revelations of a Holy Journey. Colorado Springs, CO: Navpress.

5. Picture to ponder adapted from: Ashbrook, R. T. (2014) Presence: What if Jesus Were Really Here?. USA: R. Thomas Ashbrook.

6. Nouwen, H: 1995, 'Moving from Solitude to Community to Ministry', Leadership: A Practical Journal for Church Leaders, vol. XVI, no. 2, pp. 80.

7. Skinner, B. W. (2006) The Circle of Love: Meditations by Betty W. Skinner. Marietta, GA: Tumbleweeds Productions L.L.C.

8. Nouwen, H. (1994) The Return of the Prodigal Son: A Story of Homecoming. GB: Darton, Longman & Todd.

9. Skinner, B. W. (2006) The Hidden Life: Revelations of a Holy Journey. Colorado Springs, CO: Navpress.

10		Loder, T. (1981) Guerillas of Grace: Prayers for the Battle. Minneapolis, MN: Augsburg Fortress. Used with permission.
11		Voskamp, A. (2013) The Greatest Gift: Unwrapping the Full Love Story of Christmas. Carol Stream, IL: Tyndale House Publishers.
12		Voskamp, A. (2013) The Greatest Gift: Unwrapping the Full Love Story of Christmas. Carol Stream, IL: Tyndale House Publishers.
13		Loder, T. (1981) Guerillas of Grace: Prayers for the Battle. Minneapolis, MN: Augsburg Fortress. Used with permission.
14		Loder, T. (1981) Guerillas of Grace: Prayers for the Battle. Minneapolis, MN: Augsburg Fortress. Used with permission.
15		Skinner, B. W. (2006) The Circle of Love: Meditations by Betty W. Skinner. Marietta, GA: Tumbleweeds Productions L.L.C.
16		Loder, T. (1981) Guerillas of Grace: Prayers for the Battle. Minneapolis, MN: Augsburg Fortress. Used with permission.
17		Tensen, D. (2021) The Saving I Need. Brisbane: Poetry Chapel Press. Used with permission.
18		Maglaras, F. (2021) How to Find Love in the Dark. Brisbane: Poetry Chapel Press. Used with permission.
19		Davis, N. (2000) Love Finds a Way: Little Reflections and Meditations from its Encounters. Thornleigh: Shekinah Creative Ministry Co-op. Used with permission.
20		Skinner, B. W. (2006) The Hidden Life: Revelations of a Holy Journey. Colorado Springs, CO: Navpress.

21 Loder, T. (2013) My Heart in my Mouth. Eugene, OR: Wipf and Stock Publishers. Used by permission of Wipf and Stock Publishers, www.wipfandstock.com.

22 Nouwen, H. (2007) Bread for the Journey: A Daybook for Wisdom and Faith. USA: HarperCollins.

23 Skinner, B. W. (2006) The Circle of Love: Meditations by Betty W. Skinner. Marietta, GA: Tumbleweeds Productions L.L.C.

24 Skinner, B. W. (2006) The Circle of Love: Meditations by Betty W. Skinner. Marietta, GA: Tumbleweeds Productions L.L.C.

25 Taken from: Keller, T (2024) 'Self-Control (Part 2)', *Timothy Keller Sermons Podcast by Gospel in Life*. [Podcast]. Available at: Apple Podcasts. (Accessed: 27 November 2024).

26 Skinner, B. W. (2006) The Circle of Love: Meditations by Betty W. Skinner. Marietta, GA: Tumbleweeds Productions L.L.C.

27 Tensen, D. (2020) The Wrestle. Abbotsford, BC: St Macrina Press. Used with permission.

28 Taken from: Keller, T (2024) 'Self-Control (Part 1)', *Timothy Keller Sermons Podcast by Gospel in Life*. [Podcast]. Available at: Apple Podcasts. (Accessed: 27 November 2024).

29 Skinner, B. W. (2006) The Circle of Love: Meditations by Betty W. Skinner. Marietta, GA: Tumbleweeds Productions L.L.C.

ABOUT THE AUTHORS

Dale Jones is a qualified physiotherapist and counsellor. She is married, with four adult children and enjoys supporting people through conversations that nurture a deeper understanding of self and relationships.

Alison Tye started her working life as a software engineer, and in mid-life, retrained as a spiritual director. She is married, with three children and enjoys creating spaces where others might encounter the Divine.

Dale and Alison have run retreats together for many years and share a desire for themselves and others to grow deeper in their relationship with God

www.ingramcontent.com/pod-product-compliance
Lightning Source LLC
Chambersburg PA
CBHW070736020526
44118CB00035B/1374